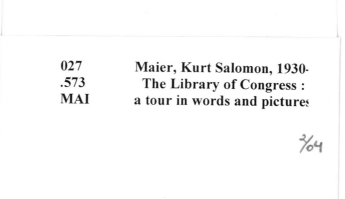

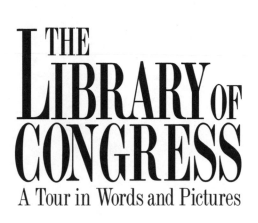

THE LIBRARY OF CONGRESS

A Tour in Words and Pictures

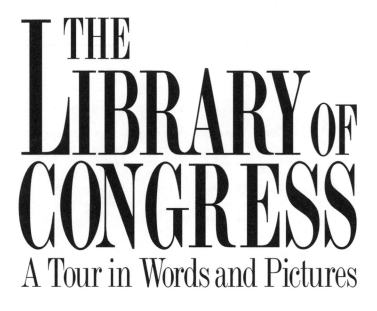

THE
LIBRARY OF
CONGRESS

A Tour in Words and Pictures

KURT S. MAIER

GRAMERCY BOOKS
New York

This 2000 edition is published by Gramercy Books™, an imprint of Random House Value Publishing, Inc., 280 Park Avenue, New York, N.Y. 10017

Gramercy Books™ and design are trademarks of Random House Value Publishing, Inc.

Random House
New York • Toronto • London • Sydney • Auckland
http://www.randomhouse.com/

Interior Design: Karen Ocker Design, New York

Printed and bound in the United States of America

Library of Congress Cataloging-in-Publication Data

Maier, Kurt Salomon, 1930–
    The Library of Congress : a tour in words and pictures / Kurt S. Maier.
        p. cm.
        Includes bibliographical references and index.
    ISBN 0-517-16249-0
    1. Library of Congress—History—Miscellanea. 2. Library of Congress—Guidebooks.
3. Library of Congress Thomas Jefferson Building (Washington, D.C.) 4. Library of Congress
John Adams Building (Washington, D.C.) 5. Library of Congress James Madison Memorial
Building (Washington, D.C.) 6. National librarians—United States—Biography. 7. Washington
(D.C.)—Buildings, structures, etc. I. Title.

Z733.U6 M187 2000
027.573—dc21

                                                                            00-038654

    8 7 6 5 4 3 2 1

President [McKinley] has referred...to my connection
with the magnificent new library building at Washington...
"the book palace of the American people," in which...the
works of all of you will be welcomed and forever preserved...

Ainsworth Rand Spofford, speech to the Literary Club, 1899

To all visitors, researchers,

and

colleagues

at

The Library of Congress

ACKNOWLEDGMENTS

Two people were invaluable in preparing this book. My wife Margery formatted numerous revisions with great attention to detail. My friend James R. Dalton edited all the revisions and stayed with the project from beginning to end.

A large debt of gratitude goes to the Manuscript Reading Room staff who put up with endless requests without losing their humor: Fred Baumann, Ernest J. Emrich, Jeffrey Flannery, Bradley Gernand, Ahmed-Jahmal Johnson, William Mobley, Josephus Nelson, and Mary Wolfskill.

The Library's Publishing Office gave me access to their outstanding reference collection and picture files. Evelyn Sinclair advised me on publishing conventions and coordinated photograph requirements: both she and Margaret Wagner read the manuscript and left many thoughtful notations. Blaine Marshall located photographs. W. Ralph Eubanks guided me through negotiations with Random House.

The Prints and Photographs Division provided extensive picture files to facilitate my selections. Yvonne Brooks of the Photoduplication Service patiently answered questions and attended to photograph orders. My colleague George von Rautenfeld of History and Literature Cataloging Division gave his sound advice on different versions of the text. Frank Evina enabled my search for historic and photographic material on the Copyright Office. Sylvia Amorin of the Visitor Services Office put me in touch with Library Docents who provided fresh insight into Library history. Ambassador William Edmondson, in particular, gave new perspective on Library artwork.

Special thanks go to sculptor Ed Dwight and to Geraldine Freund for permission to photograph his bronze of Ella Fitzgerald, which Ms. Freund recently donated to the Library. Susan Clermont of the Library's Music Division clarified many questions. Dr. Alan Fern kindly permitted reproduction of his Library Seal doodles. Edwin H. Blashfield's photograph is by permission of the Archives of American Art, Smithsonian Institution (E. H. Blashfield papers). The picture of Bob Hope is courtesy of Bob Hope Enterprises, Inc. Alex Pohl photographed both the Fitzgerald bronze and the Coca-Cola label. Christina Tyler and Robert Sokol also graciously provided photographs.

Finally, my thanks to Editor-in-Chief Susanne Jaffe and to Editor Donna Lee Lurker of Random House Value Publishing.

TABLE OF CONTENTS

LIST OF ILLUSTRATIONS

The publication of this book in the year 2000 coincides with the Bicentennial of the Library of Congress—200 years since the founding of America's oldest national cultural institution. In two centuries, the Library grew from 740 books in a small room in the Capitol to become the largest book palace in the world.

This book is written in response to questions asked by visitors to the Library of Congress. To that extent, Library tourists themselves have provided its framework by their desire to know more about the world's largest Library.

In compiling it, I have drawn from many years' experience as an on-call tour guide. Leading visitors through three Library buildings, twenty reading rooms, and numerous exhibits has been more of a pleasure for me than a chore as I have learned as much from Library visitors as they have learned about the Library.

This book was also inspired in part by four pioneering works: William Dawson Johnston's *History of the Library of Congress;* Frederick W. Ashley's *History of the Library of Congress;* David C. Mearns's *The Story Up to Now;* and John Y. Cole's *For Congress and the Nation.*

As is often the case when researching, the more I delved into the Library's history, the further the bits and pieces led me. The original work, which was envisioned as a short question-and-answer guide, expanded. It is hoped that with the arrangement of short paragraphs and varied topics, readers will pick and choose what appeals to their palates. For those who do not have an opportunity to visit the Library, this book will provide information on accessing the Library's unrivaled databases from home.

At the outset, it may be appropriate to answer the two questions most frequently asked by Library visitors: "Does the Library have a copy of every book published?" and

"How many books are in the Library?"

The answer to the first question is "No." If the Library kept a copy of every book published, it would have run out of space long ago. Certain categories of books, such as textbooks below college level, are not retained. Most books on agriculture go to the National Agricultural Library and medical books to the National Library of Medicine. Current policy is to retain about two-thirds of works submitted for copyright. As of 2000, there were approximately 19 million books in the Library's collections.

Kurt S. Maier

When did the Library of Congress buildings receive their present names?

The original Library of Congress Building or Main Building was renamed the Thomas Jefferson Building when the James Madison Memorial Building was completed in 1980. The Annex was renamed the John Adams Building.

What is the best way to see the Library of Congress?

Guided tours are given daily except Sundays and holidays. Large groups should book ahead. A continuous film providing an overview of the Library is shown in the Jefferson Building and is recommended viewing before a tour. For information on visiting the Library, call 202-707-9779.

Who was the first Library tour guide?

John Beckley (first Librarian) was also the first tour guide. In June 1804, he conducted a tour of the Library, Senate chamber, and view from the top of the Capitol. His party included German explorer Alexander von Humboldt, painter Charles Willson Peale, and Anthony Fothergill, M.D., of England who wrote a treatise on mineral water.

Who was one of the Library's most memorable tour guides?

With his mustache, tweed suit, and Windsor knot, Brian Willson was a familiar sight in the Great Hall in the 1970's and 1980's. Towering over most visitors, he explained American history in impeccable Oxford English. He looked like a British colonel from a war film and had indeed been an officer in His Majesty's Service. No matter how many times he conducted tours, he always said: "There are places in the Library of Congress yet to be discovered."

What did librarians show Raisa Gorbachev on her visit to the Library for the opening of a Russian exhibit in 1990?

The wife of the president of the Soviet Union was startled to be shown a microfiche copy of her 1967 dissertation on social aspects of daily life on collective farms in Russia.

What was the first exhibition held at the Library?

According to the *National Intelligencer* (March 2, 1830), the first exhibition displayed oriental manuscripts collected by William B. Hodgson, consul-general at Algiers.

Where do Library tunnels lead?

Tunnels connect the Jefferson, Madison, and Adams buildings. From the Madison Building, a tunnel leads to the Cannon House Office Building and from there to other congressional buildings and the Capitol. Congressional buildings on Capitol Hill are also linked by a subway on which visitors may ride. The subway, however, does not connect with the Library.

Librarian Mumford escorts Jackie Kennedy who was dressed down by a small-town newspaper when they thought her shiny silk outfit was leather.

Who may use the Library?

The Library is open to all researchers, American or foreign. A photo I.D. or other identification will be requested and a reader registration card must be obtained to do research. The User Card will contain the name, digitized photograph, and signature of the researcher. Registration and photo session last from ten to fifteen minutes. Students at high-school level and below may visit exhibits but are not admitted to the reading rooms.

Whom does the Library serve?

The first priority of the Library of Congress is to serve the information and research needs of Congress. But over the past two hundred years in serving all branches and departments of the federal government, it has become the national library of all Americans.

What books did early legislators use before the Library was established?

Members of the third session of the First Congress held in Philadelphia in 1791 used books from the city's Library Company. They also authorized the purchase of fifty volumes, including Dr. Benjamin Rush's work on the Philadelphia yellow fever epidemic, Blackstone's classic law commentaries, Jedediah Morse's *American Geography,* and Robert Burns's *Poems.* President Washington wrote to thank the Library Company for their help to the First Congress.

Who proposed the first list of books for a Congressional Library?

As representative to the Continental Congress and chairman of a committee, James Madison compiled a nine-page list of books for a future Congressional Library. His report was not acted upon, most likely because the country was at war with England and had more immediate matters to consider. Madison proposed the purchase of 550 titles in 1,300 volumes. The titles were almost exclusively devoted to history, politics, and languages. The first item was for a French encyclopedia that was finally published in 166 volumes.

Who first introduced legislation to establish a Library of Congress?

On June 23, 1790, Congressman Elbridge Gerry of Massachusetts proposed establishing a Library of Congress but his proposal was rejected. Elbridge Gerry is still remembered by the term "gerrymander," which means to divide a voting district in an unfair way to favor one political party.

When was the Library of Congress founded?

On April 24, 1800, President John Adams founded the Library of Congress by signing a bill appropriating $5,000 to purchase congressional books. On January 26, 1802, President Thomas Jefferson signed legislation formally establishing the role of the Library and appointing a Librarian of Congress. The Library may be considered Jefferson's brainchild.

How much excitement did the establishment of the Library create among members of Congress?

Not one of the five congressmen reporting on the session in which Congress established the Library even mentioned it.

How many books did the Library list in its first catalog?

The first catalog issued in 1802 cited 964 books and nine maps.

Where were they purchased?

From London booksellers Cadell & Davies who shipped them to America in eleven hair trunks, which were covered with hides from which the hair had not been removed.

Who oversees the Library?

The Joint Committee on the Library established in 1802 oversees the Library and allocates its budget. The Library Committee is the oldest joint committee of Congress.

Who serves on the committee?

The committee is composed of representatives and senators.

Spell Check: The Joint Committee on the Library ordered a book on February 8, 1841, directing that "the Librarian purchase from the agent of Mr. Webster, a copy of Webster's English Dictionary for the use of the Library."

What were some other activities of the committee?

Until the Civil War, the committee monitored daily Library activities. All decisions on purchasing books, accepting donated books, fixing salaries, and hiring staff were made by the committee without consulting the Librarian.

What famous painter was featured in an early Library exhibit?

On January 9, 1840, the committee voted to grant permission for the Library to exhibit portraits of the first five U.S. presidents by Gilbert Stuart. The portraits were owned by Mr. Phelps of Boston.

What did a rainmaker ask the committee?

In 1860, J. C. Edwards, M.D., of Sussex County, Virginia, asked the committee for congressional permission to test the practicality of producing rain by discharging one hundred cannons simultaneously, using electrical wires.

What future U.S. president served on the committee?

Rutherford B. Hayes served two years on the committee until he resigned from Congress in 1867.

What was the Library's budget in its early years?

In 1811, President James Madison approved a library budget of $1,000 for each of the next five years. In 1815, a budget appropriation of $10,000 was recommended to purchase books and maps.

Where was the Library first located?

The Library was housed in a special room in the U.S. Capitol.

Why did congressmen jump up and down on the Library roof?

Congressmen tested the roof to see how much plaster would fall from the ceiling below. They were reacting to Capitol architect Benjamin H. Latrobe's 1806 report to President Jefferson on structural defects in the Capitol wing occupied by the Library.

Fanny on the Hill: In her description of the Library housed in the Capitol, Fanny Trollope, mother of the novelist, wrote in 1828: "A very handsome room, opening on a noble stone balcony, is fitted up as a library for the members. The collection, as far as a very cursory view could enable me to judge, was very like that of a private English gentleman, but with less Latin, Greek, and Italian. This room also is elegantly furnished; rich Brussels carpet; library tables, with portfolios of engravings; abundance of sofas, and so on. The view from it is glorious, and it looks like the abode of luxury and taste." Fanny Trollope, *Domestic Manners of the Americans* (London: Penguin Books, 1997), 173.

What happened to the Library in 1814?

British troops burned the Capitol on August 24, 1814 in retaliation for an American raid in 1813 on York (now Toronto) in which the Parliament buildings with their library and archives were burned. The congressional fire destroyed the entire Library collection of books and maps. Approximately 3,000 volumes were lost.

Who else was blamed for the loss of the Library?

Patrick Magruder (second Librarian), though on sick leave at the time, was accused of negligence. His resignation was also due to financial irregularities.

What book was returned to the Library after 126 years?

Perhaps the only book to have survived the burning of the Capitol and its Library by British forces in 1814 was returned in January 1940 by rare book dealer Dr. A. S. W. Rosenbach. Entitled *An Account of the Receipts and Expenditures of the United States for the Year 1810*, the volume was originally in the President's Room of the Capitol. Three inscriptions in the book record its history: Admiral George Cockburn wrote that he had saved it and that he had given it to his brother who was governor of Bermuda. Rosenbach recorded its return to the Library.

How long did it take to restock the Library?

In 1815, the House voted 81 to 71 to buy the library of Thomas Jefferson for almost $24,000. This 6,487-volume collection was the finest of its kind in the United States. Congressman Daniel Webster opposed the purchase.

Who voted against the Jefferson purchase?

Jefferson's leanings toward France during the Revolution angered the pro-British Federalists in Congress. Consequently, those members of Congress voted unanimously against the purchase of his library. As Representative Cyrus King of Massachusetts noted: "the [Jefferson] library contained irreligious and immoral books, works of the French philosophers, who caused and influenced the volcano of the French Revolution, which had desolated Europe and extended to this country."

What other contribution did Jefferson make to the Library?

Jefferson proposed how the books should be classified. He modeled his classification system on Francis Bacon's table of science. The three Baconian divisions of History, Philosophy, and Fine Arts were subdivided into forty chapters. By the 1890's, Jefferson's classification system was no longer adequate for the Library's size.

> **Temporary Quarters:** Blodgett's Hotel, also known as the Lottery Hotel, was partially completed before 1800 on the north side of E Street N.W., between Seventh and Eighth Streets. Subsequently, it became in turn the first theater in Washington, the first home of the Federal Post Office, the first quarters of the U.S. Patent Office, a temporary meeting place of Congress, and the first place occupied by the Library of Congress after Thomas Jefferson's library was purchased in 1815.

How were Jefferson's books brought to Washington?

Approximately 27,038 pounds of books in pine bookcases were brought from Monticello to Washington by eleven wagons holding 2,458 pounds each. The wagons took seven days to reach Washington and six days to return at a cost of $56 each.

> **Nineteenth-Century Transportation Fees:** Joseph Dougherty, the man in charge of the wagons carrying Jefferson's books, listed his daily expenses as follows: "horse-hire, $1.25 per day; breakfast, $0.50; dinner, $0.75; supper and lodging, $0.75; four gallons oats and hay, $0.87; expense per day, $4.12."
>
> **Nineteenth-Century Transcription Fees:** A Miss Carroll was paid ten cents per one hundred words to transcribe a two-volume edition of Thomas Jefferson's papers. The Librarian's account book for December 24, 1850 records that she received a total of $180.90 for copying 180,295 words.

When was a separate building for the Library first proposed?

In 1817, a Senate resolution to move the Library to its own building failed to pass. In 1871, Librarian Ainsworth Rand Spofford proposed that Congress build a separate Library building; in 1888, his request was granted and construction began.

What Americans almost destroyed the Library?

On December 22, 1825, Capitol guards refused to believe Congressman Edward Everett who had seen a strange light in the Library window. One hour later when the guards agreed that something was amiss, the Library's gallery was in cinders but most of the books (like the Capitol itself) had been spared. Mr. Everett gave the less memorable address at Gettysburg in 1863.

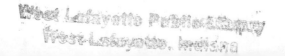

What happened on Christmas Eve 1851?

On Christmas Eve 1851, defective chimney flues destroyed 35,000 out of a total of 55,000 books, including two-thirds of Jefferson's library. Firefighters arrived with a frozen hose, which had to be taken to a gas factory on the canal to be thawed. It was a major disaster.

What other treasures were lost in the fire?

Newspapers reported the destruction of Gilbert Stuart's paintings of the first five presidents; two original portraits of Columbus; one portrait each of Bolivar, Cortez, and Baron De Kalb; a dozen French bronze medals; a statue of Jefferson; an Apollo in bronze by Mills; and a bust of Lafayette by David.

What valuable American book was saved from the fire of 1851?

John James Audubon's *Birds of America* was in the Library Committee Room at the time of the fire and was untouched by the flames. Librarian Meehan wrote afterwards: "Our copy is one of the very best; it having been selected for us by Mr. Audubon, and bound in the most substantial manner for us, under his own care and supervision."

Why did the Library's books get covered with soot during the Civil War?

Smoke from ovens in the Capitol basement penetrated the Library. Ovens had been installed to bake bread for troops stationed in Washington. A total of 8,400 loaves were baked each day. After appeals from the Librarian, President Lincoln ordered the ovens removed and a smoke-free environment was restored.

Civil War Reparations: Almost eighty years after the Civil War, the Library was ordered to replace books taken by federal officers from the Beaufort Library Society of Beaufort, South Carolina. Since these books had been destroyed by fire at the Smithsonian Institution, Congress ordered its own Library to redress the loss with duplicate books.

What was emblazoned over the Library at the conclusion of the Civil War?

A cloth with the biblical inscription "This is the Lord's doing. It is marvelous in our eyes" was displayed on the western portico. It was backlit by gas and could be seen from a great distance.

Who ordered the cloth to be set over the Library?

Benjamin Brown French (1800–70), Clerk of the House of Representatives. He was later Commissioner of Public Buildings under three presidents and sat on the podium when Lincoln spoke at Gettysburg.

Aside from congressmen, who else had borrowing privileges in the Library's early years?

In 1802, the president, vice president, and Supreme Court justices were allowed to take books from the Library.

How did President Monroe sign the Library ledger?

President Monroe placed the letters "P.U.S." after his name on the Library ledger to indicate "President of the United States."

Why was President Lincoln's Library book two years overdue?

He needed a volume on military science and kept it for two years during the Civil War.

What did President Wilson read to relax?

He had an insatiable appetite for crime novels. As a matter of fact, on November 14, 1914, the superintendent of the Library's Reading Room, William Warner Bishop, sent him the following letter: "Sir: Unless our records are in error, the books listed below have been in your possession for more than one month. If you have concluded your use of them, we shall be glad to have our messenger call for them—or such volumes as you may designate—on receipt of notification, either by mail or telephone that they are ready." The enclosed list revealed that twenty-four books were due.

What was the strangest scheme ever proposed for an expanded Library?

It was once proposed to raise the Capitol dome fifty feet to create Library space.

When did the Library move to a separate building?

On July 31, 1897, the Library in the Capitol was closed. Beginning on August 2, each of 787,715 volumes and 218,340 pamphlets was hand-carried to what is now the Jefferson Building. Not an item was lost.

What major war was concluded with a peace conference at the Library?

In June 1905, Russian and Japanese delegates met at the Library to conclude the Russo-Japanese War.

Who was the first president ever to deliver an address at the Library?

President Truman spoke on May 17, 1950 at the ceremony marking the publication of the first volume of *The Papers of Thomas Jefferson* by Princeton University Press.

Why did both houses of Congress meet in the Library's Coolidge Auditorium?

They met there on February 1, 1951 to hear General Dwight D. Eisenhower address some 400 senators and representatives on NATO and Europe's rebirth and "spirit to resist." In the afternoon, Eisenhower appeared before a closed session of the Senate Foreign Relations and Armed Services Committee.

General Eisenhower at the Coolidge Auditorium addresses a rare Joint Session of Congress held at the Library in 1951.

How many Librarians of Congress have there been?

James H. Billington became the thirteenth Librarian in 1987.

The list includes:

John Beckley	(1801-1807)	Herbert Putnam	(1899–1939)
Patrick Magruder	(1807–1815)	Archibald MacLeish	(1939–1944)
George Watterson	(1815–1829)	Luther H. Evans	(1945–1953)
John Silva Meehan	(1829–1861)	L. Quincy Mumford	(1954–1974)
John G. Stephenson	(1861–1864)	Daniel J. Boorstin	(1975–1987)
Ainsworth Rand Spofford	(1865–1897)	James H. Billington	(1987–)
John Russell Young	(1897–1899)		

Who appoints the Librarian?

The president with "the advice and consent of the Senate" appoints the Librarian.

What presidents appointed more than one Librarian?

Jefferson, Lincoln, and McKinley appointed two Librarians each.

What qualifications are necessary for the position?

There are no specified qualifications.

How long does the Librarian serve?

There is no specified term. It can be an office for life but some Librarians have resigned or been dismissed. Librarian Herbert Putnam (eighth Librarian) at his thirtieth anniversary celebration remarked to guests that he wondered if the celebration meant he was being "shelved." As it turned out, he got a reprieve for ten more years.

What Librarian served under the most presidents?

John Silva Meehan (fourth Librarian) served under nine presidents (1829–1861). Herbert Putnam (eighth Librarian) served under eight (1899–1939).

What Librarians were not born in the United States?

John Beckley (first Librarian) was born in England. John Russell Young (seventh Librarian) was born in Ireland.

What Librarians' families were related?

The wife of George Watterston (third Librarian) was a cousin of Patrick Magruder (second Librarian).

What Librarians were at the Battle of Bull Run?

Ainsworth Rand Spofford (sixth Librarian) and John Russell Young (seventh Librarian). Both were reporters, Spofford for the *Cincinnati Daily Commercial* and Young for the *Philadelphia Press*.

What Librarians won the Pulitzer Prize?

Archibald MacLeish won twice for poetry and once for drama. Daniel J. Boorstin won for history.

What Librarians were Rhodes scholars at the same Oxford college?

Daniel J. Boorstin (twelfth Librarian) and James H. Billington (thirteenth Librarian) both earned doctorates at Balliol College, Oxford University.

JOHN BECKLEY

Who was the first Librarian of Congress?

John James Beckley, elected Clerk of the House of Representatives in 1789, was appointed by President Jefferson as the first Librarian in 1802. Beckley still retained his position as Clerk. His Library salary was two dollars a day.

What key American document did Beckley sign?

John Beckley as Clerk of the House signed the Bill of Rights along with the Speaker of the House and the vice president.

How did he come to America?

Beckley, born in England on August 4, 1757, was sent to Virginia before his twelfth birthday to work as a company scribe.

What was he like?

A fine speaker, he was friends with Jefferson, Madison, and Monroe. Politically astute, he was Clerk of the Virginia senate at 20, Clerk of the Virginia House of Delegates at 21, and mayor of Richmond at 26. There is no known portrait of him.

Why was he often in debt?

He supported his parents and brother in England; a sister, mother-in-law, and two brothers-in-law in Virginia. He was also over extended in land holdings and covering loans to his friends.

Was the office of Librarian a significant post in Beckley's day?

In Beckley's day, the office of Librarian was only part-time work. His first catalog printed in 1802 listed Library holdings at 964 volumes and nine maps. Beckley began filling the shelves by appealing to the vanity of American writers and telling them that sending copies of their works to the Library would make them famous.

How long was his tenure?

Five years (1802–07).

What was his tenure like?

Beckley was embarrassed when suppliers shipped Library books with wine for President Jefferson and charged them to the same account. He was humiliated when a clerk he fired for crossing him claimed unjustly that Beckley had withheld wages. He was also upset when the House reassigned the Library to a leaky committee room and Speaker of the House Nathaniel Macon threatened to repeal the law establishing it.

What happened to Beckley?

He died in office on April 8, 1807 at the age of 50. He left his wife and son penniless. Twenty-eight years later, his debts were settled and his son inherited a large piece of land that soon became Beckley, West Virginia, named after the first Librarian of Congress.

PATRICK MAGRUDER

Where was Patrick Magruder (second Librarian) born?

On his father's estate in Maryland (1768).

What was he like?

Illness made him leave Princeton without a degree. Through persistence, he became a lawyer, ran for a House seat three times, and married three times.

What counties did he represent in Congress?

He represented Montgomery County and Frederick County, Maryland, from 1804 to 1806. In 1807, he was elected to succeed John Beckley as Clerk of the House of Representatives. Eleven days later, President Jefferson appointed him Librarian of Congress.

During his tenure, what fines did congressmen pay for books returned late?

Three dollars a day for a very large book; two dollars for a medium-size book; and one dollar for a small one. These are extraordinary fines even today.

What happened to Magruder when British troops burned the Capitol in 1814?

Fire destroyed his records of administering the Library budget.

How did Congress react to the loss of his records?

Congress duly noted that all other departments managed to save their records; that Magruder was conveniently out sick on the day of the fire; and that reconstruction of Library records from Treasury duplicates showed that he could not account for $20,000 out of the $50,000 the Library had received.

How did Magruder reply to these innuendos?

Magruder resigned as Clerk of the House of Representatives (and thus as Librarian of Congress) on January 28, 1815. He claimed that he had been found guilty without benefit of trial.

What was the aftermath of his resignation?

President Madison separated the offices of Clerk of the House of Representatives and Librarian of Congress. Magruder retired to his wife's home. The federal government filed suit against him for about $18,000. His wife died. The suit never came to trial. Magruder remarried a second time and died at the age of 51 on Christmas Eve, 1819. The first two Librarians of Congress had neither lived long nor served long.

Could the charge against Magruder have possibly been true?

Probably not. Congress may have still needed a scapegoat for the embarrassment of the fire. Magruder's public career, which began at 18, had up till then been exemplary.

GEORGE WATTERSTON

Where was George Watterston (third Librarian) born?

On a ship in New York Harbor (October 23, 1783).

What was he like?

Son of a Scottish architect, he became a lawyer. He was also somewhat of a dilettante who wrote novels and plays. Some thought he was the leading literary light of Washington, D. C. Others found him short-tempered and sharp-tongued. He despised his profession and called his first book (published anonymously) *The Lawyer; or, Man As He Ought Not to Be.*

Why did President Madison appoint him Librarian of Congress?

Wags said it had nothing to do with knowledge of books but the fact that Watterston had dedicated his poem "The Wanderer in Jamaica" to Dolley Madison. "Madam," he wrote, "I have presumed to address this poetical effusion to you..."

What was unusual about his tenure?

For thirteen out of fifteen years, he served alone—without the help of a single assistant.

What was his tenure like?

Watterston moved the 6,000-volumes of the Jefferson Collection three times. He was rather dismayed at having to call the attic of Blodgett's Hotel the Library of

Congress and dreamed of establishing a "Library of the United States." However, his lofty manner alienated the Library Committee.

Why did President Jackson dismiss him?

Watterston was a fervent Whig who wrote frequent editorials praising them. President Jackson cleaned house and dismissed him after fifteen years of service.

How did Watterston react?

Watterston badmouthed his successor and said John Silva Meehan was nothing more than a proofreader who put his son on Library payroll because the son lost a hand in a gunning accident. Ironically, when Meehan himself was dismissed and replaced by John G. Stephenson, the new Librarian fired most of the Library staff but retained the Law Librarian. Who was he? Meehan's son of the gunning accident.

What was the aftermath of Watterston's dismissal?

He lived under the delusion that a Whig president would reinstate him. But four Whig presidents (Harrison, Tyler, Taylor, and Fillmore) had no intention of doing that. So Watterston left the Whig party and focused on duties as secretary of the Washington National Monument Society. By his death on February 4, 1854, the monument had risen to 150 feet.

What was his legacy?

He adopted the Jefferson classification system, established the Library in fine quarters, and proved through unfortunate example that the Library of Congress is best served by staying out of politics.

J O H N   S I L V A   M E E H A N

Where was John Silva Meehan (fourth Librarian) born?

In New York City (February 6, 1790).

What was he like?

He was a short, kindly man with a sense of humor. He had done navy service in the War of 1812 and published Baptist periodicals.

Why did President Jackson appoint him Librarian of Congress?

Meehan sold his Washington paper *The United States Telegraph* to Jacksonians. This gave them a public platform. Once in the White House, President Jackson rewarded him by appointing him Librarian of Congress on May 28, 1829.

What was his tenure like?

He inherited a library of 16,000 volumes, hired a staff of five (including his son), but actually spent a good deal of his own time updating expense ledgers and checking out books to members of Congress. When new titles arrived, he entered them in supplementary lists instead of the central catalog, which made it difficult to locate a particular author.

What did he report about catching book thieves?

Meehan wrote to Senator Silas Wright on June 27, 1844 that the Library was once more in possession of books "stoled from the Capitol."

What was his greatest feat?

Serving Congress through nine administrations.

Where did he lack vision?

He had little experience building a library and passed up many opportunities to buy valuable collections.

Why did President Lincoln dismiss him?

Meehan was rumored to have Southern sympathies. President Lincoln cleaned house and dismissed him after thirty-two years of service.

What was the aftermath of his dismissal?

He took it calmly and hoped to become a Treasury Department clerk. However, he died on Capitol Hill (April 24, 1863) almost two years after losing the post for which he is remembered.

JOHN G. STEPHENSON

Where was John G. Stephenson (fifth Librarian) born?

In Lancaster, New Hampshire (March 1, 1828).

What was his profession?

John G. Stephenson was a physician. He studied at Dartmouth and got his doctorate in medicine from Castleton Medical College at the age of 21.

Why did President Lincoln appoint him Librarian of Congress?

Stephenson joined the Republican Party in Indiana and worked hard to elect Lincoln. With endorsements from the Governor of Indiana, a senator, a representative, nine physicians, and a dentist, he actively campaigned for the post and Lincoln appointed him on May 24, 1861.

Why was he willing to change professions?

As he confessed in a letter to President Lincoln, he found himself in "a pecuniary condition."

What was his tenure like?

He inherited a Library staff of seven and 70,000 books. He replaced six on the staff and added 13,000 books. He nearly halved the cost of book procurement to $1.70 per volume, including binding and transport. He valued cleanliness, order, and efficiency.

Who was his most memorable appointment?

Stephenson asked Cincinnati newspaper reporter Ainsworth R. Spofford to become his assistant.

How did Stephenson react to the Civil War?

He left the Library from time to time on active duty. In 1861, he served as surgeon to the 19th Indiana Volunteers. In 1863, he served as colonel with the Army of the Potomac and participated in three battles (Fitzhugh Crossing, Chancellorsville, and Gettysburg).

What distinction did he receive?

As aide to General Meredith of the First Brigade of the First Division, he was cited for bravery at Gettysburg.

What happened to Stephenson?

He suddenly resigned on December 22, 1864. No one knows why. He may have been expecting another post from Lincoln. When Lincoln died, Stephenson moved south and disappeared. In 1880, he worked for seven months as a clerk in the Surgeon General's office. He died in Washington, D.C. on November 12, 1883.

AINSWORTH RAND SPOFFORD

Where was Ainsworth Rand Spofford (sixth Librarian) born?

In Gilmanton, New Hampshire (September 12, 1825).

What was unique about him?

He had a photographic memory.

Why did President Lincoln appoint him Librarian of Congress?

Like his predecessor, Spofford actively campaigned for the post and sent President Lincoln endorsements from twenty-two senators and eighty-seven representatives. The president, much preoccupied with war, appointed him on December 31, 1864.

This tranquil studio portrait of Librarian Spofford gives no hint of his busy career.

What was Spofford's main goal?

To turn the Library from a congressional reading room into a national institution, "the book palace of the American people," as he called it.

How did he first come to the Library?

He was a reporter and liked to spend leisure time as a Library reader. He was noticed by Librarian Stephenson who offered him the position of Assistant Librarian. By coincidence, Dr. Stephenson's brother and Spofford were members of the Literary Club in Cincinnati, as was future president Rutherford B. Hayes.

What did Spofford think of the job offer?

Considering the pros and cons in a letter to his wife, he wrote that it would be a "congenial intellectual occupation," which would keep the "mind alert without severely taxing [its] powers."

How did he describe a former Librarian?

Writing to his wife, he described Librarian Meehan as "a very ancient fossil who has had the sinecure... for thirty years."

How long was his tenure?

He served between the terms of two assassinated presidents. Appointed by Lincoln in 1864, he stepped down during McKinley's first term in 1897. However, he stayed on as Chief Assistant Librarian and served under two Librarians until his death.

> **House Style:** Spofford may be considered a one-man precursor of the Congressional Research Service. Senators and representatives often requested him to write their speeches and clean up their grammar. When a member not noted for erudition cited statistics or backed facts with citations from law books and political tracts, others in the chamber cried, "Spofford!"

What was he like?

Spofford galloping on horseback was a familiar Washington sight. He held the reins while reading a book with his meticulous frock coat flapping behind him. During hot weather, he held an umbrella while reading. Of serious demeanor, he frowned on giving Library tours except to members of Congress and their guests. He was so dedicated to work that he seldom took vacations.

What was his tenure like?

He personally retrieved books from the shelves since, often, he was the only one who knew their location. Visitors described the Library of his era as a maze of volumes on tables, chairs, and window sills, not to mention basement floors and attic stairs. Spofford also registered copyright applications and had a mountain of paper, cash, and checks spilling from his desk. He was not the most careful Register of Copyright but reserved his photographic memory for books.

How legendary was his photographic memory?

Spofford was once consulted by General Lew Wallace for background material that would feature in the novel *Ben-Hur*. Spofford recommended the Harvard College Library and a specific text, then cited the exact shelf location and call number from memory. On another occasion, he was consulted by a Washington physician for a text on superstition in medicine. Spofford instantly wrote down a bibliography of eleven books and specific chapters all from memory.

What was his advice on the Ordinance of 1787?

Once, he was asked by a visitor to locate the Ordinance of 1787. When repeated searches did not produce the text, Spofford advised the visitor that his only recourse would be to visit Marietta, Ohio, and consult Professor Andrews. "He's the best informed man on the ordinance that I know of," said Spofford. "If he can't give it to you, I don't know where you can find it." The visitor blushed and replied, "I'm Professor Andrews."

How well did he remember facts and figures?

Washingtonians often mentioned the time Senator George Graham Vest of Missouri asked Spofford how much cotton the country had produced in 1859 and 1869. Without missing a beat, Spofford named amounts exported and amounts kept for domestic consumption for both years. "I don't know what we're going to do when the old boy dies," said Vest. "All the same, I'm going to check those figures." Senator Vest went to the Library and found that the cotton statistics Spofford cited were correct down to the bale.

How well did he know church doctrine?

Archbishop Chapelle once saw Spofford skimming through French historian Ernest Renan's eight-volume *Origins of Christianity.* The Archbishop scolded the Librarian in a good-natured way for wasting government time on church doctrine, then picked up a volume at random, and questioned him on a particular point. Spofford repeated almost word for word in French what Renan had written.

How well did Spofford serve the Speaker of the House?

Speaker of the House Tom Reed liked to show Spofford off to friends. Once, he saw Spofford reading a biography of British statesman Charles James Fox. Reed bided his time. Two years later, he visited the Library with friends and said, "Spofford, I'm interested in this Fox fellow, the English Premier, you know. Tremendous gambler, wasn't he?" Spofford cited the biography, summarized its contents, and named the exact sums Fox had lost.

What was Spofford's advice for dealing with bores?

"Receive the bore courteously but keep working. Always retain your good humor. Never say you are too busy. Never hint he should go away but go on with your own work. Gradually, the bore will take the hint and go away."

What warning did he give librarians?

"The Librarian who reads is lost." This referred to a famous Italian librarian noted for reading so extensively that he neglected his duties.

What did Spofford do to ensure that President Cleveland signed legislation for a new Library building?

Spofford stayed with the bill's sponsors on the House floor to answer any objections. No Librarian would violate such House protocol today. After passage, Spofford hurried the bill to the Senate to have it enrolled and obtain two signatures. He also hand-carried it to the White House. President Cleveland was at lunch, so Spofford sent the bill upstairs with the president's secretary. Fifteen minutes later, the bill came back with the president's "approved" written on it. It had taken Congress seventeen years to act on Spofford's recommendation to construct a separate Library and he was not about to lose another minute.

What was Spofford's greatest achievement?

He persuaded Congress to appropriate funds for the construction of that magnificent structure known as the Thomas Jefferson Building.

What were his other achievements?

He expanded the collections from 70,000 volumes to almost a million and created the monster that would challenge his successors. He secured legislation to make the Library the center of copyright registration. This fueled the dramatic rise in book collections since the Library now received two copies of all works deposited for copyright. He was also instrumental in purchasing the Peter Force library and in transferring 40,000 volumes from the Smithsonian Institution.

What did Spofford write to the wine company that tried to copyright its wine label?

> Library of Congress
> Washington
> May 12, 1866

C. I. Masten, Esq.
Kingston, Ulster Co., N.Y.

Sir:

I have received your label entered according to act of Congress for Masten's Wine Bitters, together with a bottle of said specific.

I have the honor to inform you that the act of Congress requiring Copyright matters to be transmitted to this Library does not include labels, nor is it my official duty to receive or to receipt for them, or for any goods or nostrum accompanying them. I enclose a copy of the law and remain

> Your obedient servant,
> A. R. Spofford
> Librarian

P.S. If you desire a legal protection of your exclusive right to make and send any such article, you should apply to the Patent Office.

The bottle awaits your orders.

Why did Secret Service agents visit Spofford?

In 1897, Secret Service agents visited him to ask about George Washington's diary for the year 1787, which Spofford kept in his desk. This diary, together with 350 letters from Thomas Jefferson, King George II, John Hancock, and Benedict Arnold, had been sold to a New York autograph dealer who became suspicious of the low price being asked. The dealer then alerted the Treasury Department. One of the sellers, a Library of Congress employee, claimed that he had found the diary on a stone ledge by the Capitol building.

What was Spofford's final act of dedication to the Library?

While standing at the central desk of the Main Reading Room about 1907, he crumpled to the floor. He laughed and said it was nothing and that he would be back at his post in a day or two. Six weeks later, he returned from the stroke with his left arm strapped across his chest. He died on August 11, 1908.

How did Librarian Putnam eulogize him?

A. R. S.

1825–1908

———

The Epilogue

He toiled long, well, and with Good Cheer
In the Service of Others
Giving his Whole, Asking little
Enduring patiently, Complaining
Not at all
With small Means
Effecting Much

* * *

He had no Strength that was not Useful
No Weakness that was not Lovable
No Aim that was not Worthy
No Motive that was not Pure

* * *

Ever he Bent

His Eye upon the Task

Undone

Ever he Bent

His Soul upon the Stars

His Heart upon

The Sun

*　　*

Bravely he Met

His Test

Richly he Earned

His Rest

JOHN RUSSELL YOUNG

Where was John Russell Young (seventh Librarian) born?

In Ireland (November 20, 1840).

What was his early life like?

His mother died when he was ten. He and three siblings were sent to different houses. His work as a printer at fifteen enabled him to reunite his brother and two sisters and support them. His later work for Philadelphia editor John W. Forney who became Clerk of the House of Representatives and Secretary of the Senate brought Young to Washington.

What battle did he witness as a reporter?

The Battle of Bull Run. Describing a farmyard now a makeshift hospital, he wrote: "Where roses had grown in the morning, dead men lay by noon."

What political roles did he play?

As managing editor of the *Tribune*, he led the charge to impeach President Johnson. As correspondent for the *New York Herald*, he joined the entourage of Ulysses S. Grant and covered the ex-president's travels for two-and-a-half years.

On Grant's recommendation, President Arthur appointed Young United States Minister to China where he furthered American trade.

What personal tragedies befell Young?

Two of his three children died. Then, after his return from presidential travels, he lost the last one, followed by his wife. Three years later, during his Chinese mission, he was bereaved again when his second wife died.

What connection did his secretary in Peking have with the Library?

Young's secretary in Peking, William W. Rockhill, was later appointed ambassador there and donated his personal collection of 6,000 Chinese books to the Library.

Why did President McKinley appoint Young Librarian of Congress?

Young was hoping to be appointed United States Minister to Spain. But President McKinley needed someone to begin a fresh era for the Library in its new building. By appointing Young Librarian on July 1, 1897, the president ended Spofford's thirty-three-year tenure. Ironically, Spofford who was seventy-two stayed on as Assistant Librarian for another eleven years and actually outlived both Young and McKinley.

What was Young's tenure like?

Brief. It lasted only eighteen months, the shortest tenure of any Librarian. Nonetheless, he presided over the Library's move to its first separate home, the magnificent Thomas Jefferson Building. He was also a pioneer in hiring women who composed 25 percent of his staff.

What was his legacy?

No longer the firebrand of his early editorials, he brought diplomacy and poise to his duties. A few days after taking office, he wrote:

> To do your work! Then do it!
> In sorrow! Yes—in—pain—
> In Time you'll never rue it—
> Nor eternity undo it—
> The doing is the gain.

He died in office (January 17, 1899), the second Librarian to do so.

Where was Herbert Putnam (eighth Librarian) born?

In New York City (September 20, 1861).

Who was his competition to be Librarian?

A host of hopefuls descended on the Capitol after Librarian Young died. J. C. M. Hanson in tribute to Putnam mentions "needy journalists, clergymen without a call, teachers unable to teach, unsuccessful authors, actors without engagements; but all brimful of confidence their great love of books and their literary inclinations would enable them to solve all the difficulties connected with the management of a great library."

Librarian Putnam spent forty years at this Library desk.

What were Putnam's qualifications?

A Harvard graduate, he had been librarian at the Minneapolis Athenaeum and director of the Boston Public Library.

Why did President McKinley appoint him Librarian of Congress?

President McKinley knew his father who had been a Lincoln appointee as collector of internal revenue in New York. George Palmer Putnam also founded the Putnam publishing firm. His son came easily to mind when the president sought a new Librarian of Congress. Library school professor Melvil Dewey and publisher R. R. Bowker endorsed the selection. McKinley appointed Putnam on March 13, 1899.

What was his tenure like?

It was the longest on record. Putnam served as Librarian for forty years (1899–1939) and then stayed on as the first Librarian Emeritus (1939–1955), a post authorized by Congress at $5,000 a year.

Out to Pasture: In his first Report to Congress, Putnam wrote that two horses would be needed for the Library wagon. The maintenance for the animals was budgeted at $650. As a long-term economic measure, purchase of an electric automobile for $1,845 was proposed. The vehicle could be charged without expense at the Library's power plant.

How did job seekers jockey for Library positions during the Putnam era?

Senator Augustus Bacon campaigned for a Miss Rutherford by saying that if she were hired, he would get more cataloger positions added to the Deficiency Bill. Senator Samuel D. McEnery campaigned for a Mrs. Price whose husband had assisted him during a recent illness. Forrest McKinley of the U. S. Army Hospital Department applied as a relative of the president. Putnam ran a tight ship and always looked to qualifications.

What were some exam questions for Library positions?

Starting in 1898 under Librarian Young, candidates for Library positions had to answer exam questions. Putnam continued the policy. Here are sample questions from his tests for each department :

T H E   C A T A L O G   D E P A R T M E N T

Name any reference work that you would consider of main assistance in ascertaining the facts as to the life and writings of an American author.

(a) Of an English author.

(b) Of a French author.

(c) Of a German author.

Suggest any principle that should govern in the abbreviation of titles.

What advantage has the card catalog over the printed, and, vice versa, the printed over the card catalog?

THE COPYRIGHT DEPARTMENT

State the nature of the primary and fundamentally necessary book of reference to be kept in relation to the fiscal department of the copyright office.

Draw in pencil a rough form of trial balance sheet to show the essential elements of the copyright business.

In recording titles, what errors do you find it the most necessary to guard against committing?

GENERAL SERVICE

Which of the following-named books are found on your deck: Bryce's *American Commonwealth*, Taine's *English Literature*, Henderson's *Dictionary of Plants*, Proctor's *The Sun*, Bohn's *Classical Library*, Publications of the Hakluyt Society?

Who wrote the following-named books: *The Vicar of Wakefield*, *Conquest of Mexico*, *Autocrat of the Breakfast Table*, *The Sketch Book*, *The Boys of '76*, and *Little Lord Fauntleroy*?

What do the following numbers signify as applied to the shelves on each deck: 6451, 8131, 1121?

THE GRAPHIC ARTS

What are the principal divisions of intaglio engravings?

What are the marks by which the order of print of an engraving can be told?

Explain the various mechanical processes by which the different kinds of reproduced pictures are made.

THE PERIODICAL DEPARTMENT

How would you classify a miscellaneous collection of periodicals upon various subjects?

What is the largest complete set of any one periodical in the Library and in what year does it begin?

What is the oldest newspaper in the Library?

MAPS AND CHARTS

What are roller maps? Explain how they are to be systematized in the hall of maps and charts.

Mention the names of Government departments publishing maps.

Give the various shapes in which maps are found.

THE MANUSCRIPT DEPARTMENT

What arrangement of manuscripts is adopted in the manuscript department for manuscripts relating especially to the career of an individual or to a definite period of history?

Make a calendar of Delaware State Papers, volume 11, folio 43 (16).

Who was Peter Force?

THE LIBRARY OF MUSIC

How is mechanical music classified?

Under what heads are vocal quartets arranged?

What is meant by "opus?"

How did Putnam greet new employees?

His famous line was always: "We expect great things from you!"

How did he conduct staff meetings?

Putnam remained seated and gave instructions while staff stood around his desk. No one was allowed to take notes. They were expected to concentrate on his words.

How did he conduct evening events?

He expected staff to wear tailcoats and white ties for evening events.

What was the Librarian's Round Table?

It was a dining club that met three or four times a week to discuss the arts, history, and the social sciences but not politics. Among participants were William Howard Taft, Calvin Coolidge, Franklin D. Roosevelt, H. G. Wells, and Winston Churchill. Lunch was served at 1 p.m. and women were admitted but all agreed the food was never as good as the talk.

Bread and Butter Issue: As a member of the Librarian's Round Table, Spofford was present when the question was raised whether the plate with bread and butter should be on the right side or on the left. Fifteen raised hands voted for the left and Mr. Spofford voted for the right whereupon the vote was unanimously changed to the right.

What happened when Putnam arrived at New York Harbor with the Gutenberg Bible?

Two lawyers waited dockside to serve him summons barring the Library of Congress from receiving the Bible until certain financial claims by one of the lawyers were satisfied. Putnam got wind of the arrival party and arranged for the Coast Guard to take the Bible before he docked.

Fine Distinction: Overwhelmed by the Orientalia collection, which includes Arabic, Chinese, Hebrew, Japanese, and Korean, a visitor once asked Librarian Putnam: "Are these books used extensively?" "No," replied Putnam, "They are not used extensively; they are used intensively."

What did library school professor Melvil Dewey write in his honor?

On the occasion of Putnam's thirtieth anniversary as Librarian, Dewey penned these lines. They contain examples of Dewey's spelling reforms:

So bless you, Dr. Putnam, may you liv a thousand years
To render splendid service in this vale of human tears
And may I liv a thousand, too, a thousand less a day
For I shouldn't like to be on earth and know you'd past away.

Books Over There: Following America's entry in World War I, the Library became the general headquarters for a national effort by American libraries to supply servicemen with books. Librarian Putnam as general director spent eight months in England and France in 1919. Library buildings were erected in forty training camps. At the American Expeditionary Force University in Beaune, France, a 30,000-volume library had seats for 1,500.

What was the Great Patronage Raid?

In 1933, Congressman James V. McClintic of Snyder, Oklahoma, told the press he planned to redistribute eight hundred Library positions to Democrat office seekers. He also suggested that Librarian Putnam was more than ripe for retirement. McClintic particularly objected to fifty foreign Library workers whose only skills were languages. When the press wondered if Democrats could transcribe Confucius and the Koran into English or speak Hungarian and write Sanskrit, President Franklin D. Roosevelt wisely upheld the merit system governing federal employment.

Why was Putnam denied a pension?

In 1937, the House denied him an annual pension of $7,500 on the grounds that he had earned an annual salary of $10,000, had the longest tenure of any Librarian, and had never contributed to a retirement fund. His pension was denied by a vote of 116 to 115. One congressman said Putnam earned as much as a representative but never had to spend a cent on campaigning.

What happened to Putnam?

As his fortieth anniversary approached, he let it be known that he would willingly retire if he could retain a title and half his salary. According to his wishes and in respect for many years of service, Congress, supported by President Franklin D. Roosevelt, conferred on Putnam the title of Librarian Emeritus with an honorarium of $5,000 a year. He served in the post for another sixteen years and died on August 14, 1955.

What were his greatest achievements?

He ordered the Library of Congress classification system to be developed, acquired the Gutenberg Bible, and built the Library Annex known as the John Adams Building.

MACLEISH AND WORLD WAR II

Where was Archibald MacLeish (ninth Librarian) born?

In Glencoe, Illinois (May 7, 1892).

Where was he educated?

Yale and Harvard.

What were his professions?

Lawyer, journalist, and poet.

For what did he win three Pulitzer Prizes?

He won for his poem "Conquistador" in 1932; for his *Collected Poems 1917–52* in 1953; and for his drama *J. B.* in 1959.

Why did President Franklin D. Roosevelt appoint him Librarian of Congress?

The president wanted a new deal for the Library and chose a poet. Supreme Court Justice Felix Frankfurter had been MacLeish's law professor at Harvard and highly endorsed him. Roosevelt appointed MacLeish on June 6, 1939.

Why did he delay taking office?

That summer, he "was deep into a long poem" and told the president, "I have to finish." Roosevelt agreed that he could start in the fall. The poem: "America Was Promises."

Who opposed his nomination?

In addition to the 1,400 librarians who petitioned the Senate, the president of the American Library Association said: "I have the highest respect for Mr. MacLeish as a poet, but I should no more think of him as a librarian of Congress than as chief engineer of a new Brooklyn Bridge." A congressman also attacked MacLeish on the floor of the House as a "fellow traveler of the Communist party."

Who swore MacLeish in?

On October 2, 1939, the village postmaster and notary public of Conway, Massachusetts, swore in MacLeish who had called there for his mail.

Why did the union representing Library employees welcome his appointment?

MacLeish had been editor of *Fortune* magazine and joined the American Newspaper Guild, a CIO (Congress of Industrial Organizations) affiliate. The Library's union was also represented by the CIO.

What misconception about the Library did he try to change?

As he wrote in his *Annual Report* for 1941: "There are still many members of the most learned professions who believe that the Library of Congress is a library for Congressmen only."

How did MacLeish help Nazi refugees?

He was active on the Emergency Committee in Aid of Displaced Foreign Scholars. The committee provided visas for artists, dissidents, and writers trapped in occupied Europe.

What two literary exiles did he hire at the Library?

German novelist Thomas Mann and French poet Saint-John Perse.

How did he help Thomas Mann?

MacLeish appointed Mann Consultant in Germanic Literature, a post he held from 1941 to 1950. He gave an annual lecture at the Coolidge Auditorium. Vice President Henry A. Wallace attended the first. Mann and his family had been on the Nazi wanted list.

What book found at the Library inspired Thomas Mann?

He saw a handmade German hymn book produced by the Seventh Day Baptist community in Ephrata, Pennsylvania. Benjamin Franklin had once owned the book whose

translated title is *A Perfect Specimen or Key for Each and Every Kind of Tune and Manner of Instant, Faultless. . . Singing and Harmonization* (1746). It is more commonly known as the *Ephrata Codex.* Mann described this hymnal in his novel *Doctor Faustus* (1948).

How did MacLeish help Saint-John Perse?

MacLeish appointed Saint-John Perse Consultant in French Literature, a post he held from 1941 to 1946. He then worked as Honorary Consultant from 1947 to 1953. Saint-John Perse was the penname of Alexis Saint-Léger Léger who had been a diplomat in the French Foreign Ministry and part of the delegation that negotiated face to face with Hitler at the Munich Conference in 1938. He fled France after the Nazi takeover and came to the United States.

What else did Thomas Mann and Saint-John Perse have in common?

They both won the Nobel Prize for Literature, Thomas Mann in 1929 and Saint-John Perse in 1960.

> **War Poets:** During the dark war days of 1942, Winston Churchill lent the Library the manuscript of Arthur Hugh Clough's poem, "Say Not the Struggle Naught Availeth" to be exhibited with other manuscripts of famous "Poems of Faith and Freedom."

What did a merchant seaman leave to the Library during World War II?

MacLeish received a letter from a seaman who had immigrated to the United States as a boy. The seaman willed his $5,000 life insurance to the Library to purchase books if his ship were torpedoed.

What other government posts did MacLeish hold while Librarian?

He was director of the Office of Facts and Figures (1941) and assistant director of the Office of War Information (1942). He also wrote speeches for President Franklin D. Roosevelt.

Who was the Library's man in Europe during World War II?

Manuel Sanchez was the Library's agent in neutral Spain, Portugal, and North Africa from 1943 to 1945. He procured German and Italian technical books and newspapers and sent 66,508 items to the Library for distribution to American intelligence.

What is a good example of Library support for the war effort?

In 1943, a handbook of instructions for the Luftwaffe was cataloged, bound, and sent to a federal agency within six hours of being received from Manuel Sanchez in Europe. This is one of the fastest turnaround times on Library record.

Covert Operations: During World War II, dozens of researchers from the O.S.S. (Office of Strategic Services) occupied rooms in the Library Annex (Adams Building). Research covered all aspects of the war, including sabotage, pinpointing enemy targets, psychological warfare, and identifying groups friendly to Allied forces. Only the Library with its matchless collection of maps, city and telephone directories, and other resources from occupied countries could supply the information they needed. During 1944 alone, O.S.S. staff used 14,000 books from the Library and sent 5,000 volumes to the agency's own library. Lucy Salamanca's book about the Library of Congress published during the war is appropriately entitled *Fortress of Freedom*. Here are some of the reasons why: also housed in the Annex was the Bureau of Intelligence of the Office of War Information. Located in the Jefferson Building were the Offices of the Censor from the Post Office Department and the Treasury; space was also found for the Army Map Service.

How did the Library aid intelligence during the war?

American officers consulted the Library's European city directories and railroad timetables to locate targets for bomber pilots. Allied meteorologists consulted the diaries of a Methodist minister in Burma. These diaries, donated to the Library in 1902, contained vital information on weather patterns.

What did enemy newspapers tell them?

Allied intelligence could estimate the number of casualties of enlisted men from the obituaries.

How else did the Library serve the armed forces?

In addition to collecting surplus books for servicemen and women, the Library received book requests from "War Prisoners' Aid of the YMCA" for Allied servicemen held by the Germans in 1944. From prisoner-of-war camp Stalag Luft III came requests for texts on foreign languages, algebra, Gregg Shorthand, sketching, and cartooning. What class had the highest enrollment? German conversation.

When was the Library open twenty-four hours a day?

During the war, parts of the Library remained open twenty-four hours a day for members of Congress and researchers from military and intelligence services. A twenty-four-hour teletype in the Legislative Reference Bureau provided abstracts for war agencies.

How did China use the Library during the war?

Shortly before the attack on Pearl Harbor, the Chinese government sent the Library one hundred boxes of its rarest manuscripts and printed treasures for safekeeping.

What happened during an air raid drill on Capitol Hill?

An air raid alarm sounded on a hot June day in 1943 during a concert on the Capitol steps. The entire audience rushing to the Jefferson Building caused great confusion since the Library had not been notified of the drill. The Library was twenty-third on the list of public buildings to receive notice of the alert. The Hot Shoppes (a popular cafeteria chain) was third.

What happened to the Jefferson Building's twenty-two cuspidors?

They were scrapped for the war effort.

What did film director Frank Capra request from the Library during the war?

Army Major Capra wrote to Librarian MacLeish on February 27, 1942, requesting permission for his staff of scenario writers to smoke in one of the rooms assigned to them. Capra wrote: "You know how scenario writers are. The no-smoking regulation nearly killed them."

When did prisoners of war work for the Library?

After the war, German POW's worked for the Library of Congress Mission in Europe, which was established to acquire Nazi and scientific publications and archives. The prisoners worked in civilian status and received wages and food rations since times were hard in their destroyed countries. On completing the projects, the prisoners were released.

To whom did the Library ship millions of books?

On behalf of the Veterans Administration, the Library shipped 2.2 million books in over 24,000 boxes to educational institutions throughout the country. The books were for veterans enrolled in schools. Shipments took place from 1946 to 1948 and at the time were probably the largest book distribution program in history.

What significant letter arrived at the Library forty-three years late?

In July 1984, the U.S. Postal Service in Philadelphia forwarded a letter to the Library dated December 12, 1941. It had been sent from the Japanese embassy in Washington five days after the bombing of Pearl Harbor and requested the Library to "Please send your messenger to the Japanese embassy for books which we borrowed from the Library of Congress." The postal authorities added that, since the postage was adequate for 1941, they were not charging the Library an additional fee.

How did MacLeish's successor remember him?

As "the brush of the comet."

What happened to MacLeish?

He resigned as Librarian on December 19, 1944 to assume a third government post—Assistant Secretary of State. He held the new post for eight months, resigned, and returned to teaching at Harvard and later Amherst. He died on April 20, 1982.

LUTHER EVANS

Where was Luther Evans (tenth Librarian) born?

In Sayersville, Texas (October 13, 1902).

What were his academic connections?

He received a doctorate from Stanford, taught at Dartmouth and Princeton, and later worked as library director at Columbia.

What prepared him for his role as Librarian?

He directed the Historical Records Survey for the Works Projects Administration and inventoried church and public records to improve nationwide accessibility. This experience served him well in developing basic cataloging rules for the Library's National Union Catalog of Manuscript Collections.

Why did President Truman appoint him Librarian of Congress?

He was a logical successor to Librarian MacLeish who had first named him director of the Legislative Reference Service and Chief Assistant Librarian and then Acting Librarian of Congress whenever MacLeish was away on diplomatic assignment.

What was his tenure like?

Though budgets were tight after World War II, Evans managed to expand the collections by about 28 percent.

What was his philosophy?

As he wrote in the *Sunday Star* shortly after taking office: "No spot on the earth's surface is any longer alien to the interests of the American people. No particle of knowledge should remain unavailable to them."

What was his legacy?

Evans presided over the establishment of the Legislative Reference Service as a separate function within the Library. He also created the Science Division, the Technical Information Division, two divisions for European and Slavic affairs, and a Folklore Section in the Music Division.

Why did he spend $50,000 of his own money to buy the manuscript of Alice in Wonderland?

Evans bought the manuscript of *Alice in Wonderland* at auction, raised reimbursement contributions by popular subscription, and presented the manuscript to the British Museum in 1948 to honor Britain's valiant resistance during the first years of World War II.

What is the one word that summarizes his goals?

Accessibility. He began microfilming rare manuscripts to make them more accessible to researchers. He published the Library's catalog cards in book form to make them more accessible to other libraries. He also made the Librarian of Congress a more public figure by touring the country and giving speeches.

Why did he resign as Librarian?

Evans resigned on July 1, 1953 to become director general of the United Nations Educational, Scientific, and Cultural Organization. He held the new post for five years, became director of the legal collections at Columbia University in 1962, retired ten years later, and died on December 23, 1981.

L.   QUINCY   MUMFORD

Where was L. Quincy Mumford (eleventh Librarian) born?

In Ayden, North Carolina (December 11, 1903).

What is unique about him?

Son of a tobacco farmer, this Duke graduate and skilled debater was the first Librarian of Congress with a library science degree.

Librarian Mumford surrounded by his predecessors.

What was his library experience?

He worked 16 years at the New York Public Library on Fifth Avenue where he simplified cataloging procedures. He also worked nine years at the Cleveland Public Library where he dealt skillfully with the board of trustees, the staff, the union, and the public.

Why did President Eisenhower appoint him Librarian of Congress?

The two previous Librarians (MacLeish and Evans) had often been absent to pursue outside interests. President Eisenhower felt it was time to appoint someone whose primary interest was books. As president of the American Library Association, Mumford fit the bill. Eisenhower appointed him on April 22, 1954.

What was his tenure like?

During more than twenty years in office, he saw appropriations grow tenfold to almost $97 million. Collections more than doubled to 74 million items. The Legislative Reference Service became the Congressional Research Service.

What major undertaking did he complete?

The papers of twenty-three presidents were indexed and filmed.

What new initiatives did he begin?

He began an experiment that became a permanent feature of publishing. Books could now be cataloged before they were published. This allowed their Library of Congress catalog card numbers to be printed in the books themselves. Mumford also established the Preservation Office to save unique books and films.

What is perhaps his greatest achievement?

Obtaining funding ($123 million) to construct the James Madison Building.

How is he remembered?

As the man who took library science to the future. As far back as 1966, cataloging data was already stored on computer tape for distribution to other libraries. Mumford's popularity with Congress exempted him from mandatory retirement. By the time he left office on December 31, 1974, he had brought the Library of Congress well beyond the frontier of the electronic age. He died in Washington on August 15, 1982.

D A N I E L   J .   B O O R S T I N

Where was Daniel J. Boorstin (twelfth Librarian) born?

In Atlanta, Georgia (October 1, 1914).

Where was he educated?

Harvard, Yale, and Oxford University where he was a Rhodes scholar. By 2000, he had almost fifty honorary degrees.

Why did President Ford appoint him Librarian of Congress?

Boorstin was a Senior Historian and former Director of the National Museum of History and Technology, Smithsonian Institution. He was also a 1974 Pulitzer Prize winner for *The Americans: The Democratic Experience.* He was well qualified for the post. The president appointed him on June 20, 1975.

Who opposed his nomination?

The American Library Association. Librarian MacLeish, another Pulitzer Prize winner, had also been opposed by this organization. However, the Senate confirmed Boorstin without debate. He took office on November 12, 1975.

What other major prizes did he win?

Boorstin is one of the few historians to win the triple crown of the Pulitzer Prize, the Parkman Prize, and the Bancroft Prize.

What was Librarian Boorstin's concept of the Library?

In accordance with his motto "You never know when an idea is about to be born," he opened the Library to all patrons and fostered the spirit of exploration. He conceived of the Library as the "world's greatest Multi-Media Encyclopedia."

What program is he identified with?

He created the Center for the Book, an outreach program to encourage interest in libraries and literacy. The Center now has affiliates throughout the country.

JAMES H. BILLINGTON

Where was James H. Billington (thirteenth Librarian) born?

In Bryn Mawr, Pennsylvania (June 1, 1929).

Where was he educated?

Princeton and Oxford University where he was a Rhodes scholar. By 2000, he had almost twenty-five honorary degrees.

What magazine did he found?

The *Wilson Quarterly* (1976). Dr. Billington was director of the Woodrow Wilson International Center for Scholars (1973–87) and established eight new programs there, including the Kennan Institute for Advanced Russian Studies.

Why did President Reagan appoint him Librarian of Congress?

He is a distinguished scholar and historian. The president appointed him on April 17, 1987.

What political revolution did he witness?

Fluent in Russian, he was in Moscow on August 19, 1991 when fighting broke out at the Russian Parliament between supporters of Mikhail Gorbachev and Boris Yeltsin. Dr. Billington and his staff continued their work with "business as usual" determination while coups and countercoups went on.

What television program did he write and narrate?

The Face of Russia (1998), which aired on Public Broadcasting Stations.

What is one of his major achievements so far?

Under Librarian Billington, many Library collections and exhibits have been digitized and are now available online in American homes and schools. He has become identified with bringing the Library into the Internet Age.

CONSULTANTS IN POETRY

What did the title of Consultant in Poetry to the Library of Congress mean?

The Librarian conferred this title on distinguished poets from 1937 to 1986. It entitled them to an annual stipend and office space at the Library of Congress.

How many Consultants in Poetry have there been?

This list includes:

JOSEPH AUSLANDER (1937–1941)

VACANT (1941–1943)

ALLEN TATE (1943–1944)

ROBERT PENN WARREN (1944–1945)

LOUISE BOGAN (1945–1946)

KARL SHAPIRO (1946–1947)

LÉONIE ADAMS (1948–1949)

ELIZABETH BISHOP (1949–1950)

CONRAD AIKEN (1950–1952)

VACANT (1952–1956, when William Carlos
    Williams declined to serve)

RANDALL JARRELL (1956–1958)

ROBERT FROST (1958–1959)

RICHARD EBERHART (1959–1961)

LOUIS UNTERMEYER (1961–1963)

HOWARD NEMEROV (1963–1964)

REED WHITTEMORE (1964–1965)

STEPHEN SPENDER (1965–1966)

JAMES DICKEY (1966–1968)

WILLIAM JAY SMITH (1968–1970)

WILLIAM STAFFORD (1970–1971)

JOSEPHINE JACOBSEN (1971–1973)

DANIEL HOFFMAN (1973–1974)

STANLEY KUNITZ (1974–1976)

ROBERT HAYDEN (1976–1978)

WILLIAM MEREDITH (1978–1980)

MAXINE KUMIN (1981–1982)

ANTHONY HECHT (1982–1984)

ROBERT FITZGERALD (1984–1985,
    never served due to illness)

REED WHITTEMORE (1984–1985,
    replaced Fitzgerald)

GWENDOLYN BROOKS (1985–1986)

What award did the Library deny Ezra Pound?

In 1949, the Fellows in American Letters awarded the first Bollingen Prize in Poetry to Ezra Pound for the *Pisan Cantos*. Among the thirteen Fellows deciding the award, which was administered by the Library, were Conrad Aiken, W. H. Auden, T. S. Eliot, and Katherine Anne Porter. An article in the *Saturday Review of Literature* immediately attacked Pound because he made Fascist radio broadcasts for Italy during World War II. The cantos were also attacked for lack of literary merit. Senator Theodore Green, chairman of the Joint Committee on the Library, then canceled the award with the following statement: "A Library of Congress prize carries the prestige of all the people and if its prizes do not represent all the people, the Government is bound to get into trouble." The prize was worth $1,000.

Consultant in Poetry Elizabeth Bishop seen in the office that inspired her poem describing the view of the Capitol.

POET LAUREATES

What does the title of Poet Laureate Consultant in Poetry to the Library of Congress mean?

In 1985, an act of Congress changed the title "Consultant in Poetry" to "Poet Laureate Consultant in Poetry." The first to hold the post was poet Robert Penn Warren, author of the novel, *All the King's Men*. The title change also expanded the role. Recent Poet Laureates have achieved celebrity status.

What stipend does the Poet Laureate receive?

An annual fee of $35,000, funded by gift from Archer M. Huntington.

What are the Poet Laureate's duties?

While there are no specified duties, the Poet Laureate recommends poetry collections, gives public readings, encourages the study of poetry, and on occasion composes a poem marking a significant national event.

How many Poet Laureates have there been?

The list includes:

ROBERT PENN WARREN (1986–1987)	MONA VAN DUYN (1992–1993)
RICHARD WILBUR (1987–1988)	RITA DOVE (1993–1995)
HOWARD NEMEROV (1988–1990)	ROBERT HASS (1995–1997)
MARK STRAND (1990–1991)	ROBERT PINSKY (1997–2000)
JOSEPH BRODSKY (1991–1992)	

What emphasis have recent Poet Laureates brought to the position?

Rita Dove brought together writers to explore the African-American experience. Robert Pinsky gathered a cross section of Americans reading their favorite poems as part of the Library's Bicentennial.

THE THOMAS JEFFERSON BUILDING

What was on Capitol Hill in pre-colonial times?

Archaeologists found remains of an Indian village where the Jefferson Building now stands.

What did the Sage of Baltimore have to say about the Library?

"Such is the Library of Congress, an oasis of public usefulness in a town of quacks and grafters. Its gaudy building is known to every visitor in Washington; thousands of gaping tourists plod through it every day, staggered and benumbed by the gorgeous hand-painted frescoes and barber-shop mosaics. But not many of them linger to imbibe at its Pierian spring, and very few ever think to remember it when they make their wills." H. L. Mencken, "The Library of Congress," *Baltimore Evening Sun* (December 20, 1926).

What does the fountain in front of the Jefferson Building show?

The fountain depicts Neptune, god of the sea, with Triton (a minor sea god), a nymph, frogs, turtles, sea monsters, and a sea horse. Neptune is seated and would be twelve feet high standing. Seven water jets issue from the jaws of the monsters.

Who were the original architects of the Library of Congress?

John L. Smithmeyer and Paul J. Pelz beat twenty-seven competitors and were awarded first prize of $1,500 in the contest for best design of a Congressional Library. Smithmeyer (1832–1908) was born in Austria and Pelz (1841–1918) was from Germany. Smithmeyer was the architect in charge.

Why did Smithmeyer and Pelz not complete construction of the Library?

In 1888, Congress appointed Brigadier General Thomas Lincoln Casey (1831–1896) to oversee completion of the Library. Casey was the Army's chief of engineers and had overseen completion of the Washington Monument, as well as the Old Executive

Office Building (formerly the State, War, and Navy Building), next to the White House. He promptly replaced Smithmeyer with Pelz and appointed his own son, Edward Pearce Casey (1864–1940), a West Point graduate, to complete the interior artwork. Edward Casey was also known for designing the Connecticut Avenue Bridge and the Continental Memorial Hall for the Daughters of the American Revolution, both in Washington. In 1892, General Casey dismissed Pelz for mental instability and appointed Edward Casey as architect.

What happened to Smithmeyer and Pelz after being fired?

Smithmeyer and Pelz sued the government for breach of contract and claimed in damages three percent of the total cost of the Library Building, then valued at $7 million. The U.S. Supreme Court upheld the opinion of the Court of Claims and awarded them $48,000. On July 28, 1898, Smithmeyer was found trying to load a revolver on a settee in the gallery above the Main Reading Room. He was disarmed, arrested, and saved from an apparent suicide attempt. Later, on trying to reclaim his revolver from the captain of the watch, he was told that he had been banned from ever appearing in the building again. Pelz was treated for mental disturbances.

What other buildings did Smithmeyer and Pelz design?

Smithmeyer and Pelz also designed the Academic Building at Georgetown University in Washington, the Carnegie Library and Music Hall in Allegheny, Pennsylvania, and the U.S. Army and Navy Hospital in Hot Springs, Arkansas.

Who was the Superintendent of Construction while the Library was being built?

Bernard R. Green (1843–1914) was involved more than any other man in the day-to-day construction of the Library. He spent twenty-six years at the Library, fourteen of them in planning, constructing, and operating the building. He also supervised construction of the Washington Monument, the Old Executive Office Building, and the New York Public Library.

What was the oddest request received by building engineer Green?

Congressman Benjamin F. Marsh requested that Green allow the congressman's small son to set up a stand to sell things on the corner by the Library. An equally curious request came from Representative H. W. Blair objecting "to any and all trees within the Library grounds."

What was placed in the cornerstone of the Jefferson Building?

On August 28, 1890, the chief cornerstone was laid in the northeast corner. Placed inside the copper box were: annual reports of the Librarian of Congress (1872–1888); annual reports of the chief of engineers (1888–1889); photographs of the building site on August 15, 1890; legislative acts for the erection of the building; the *Congressional Directory* (for May 1890); the *American Almanac* for 1889; and two Washington and two New York City newspapers.

How much cement was used to construct the Library?

The cement filled 73,000 barrels.

Why is the site of the Jefferson Building associated with Lincoln?

Congressman Lincoln and his family lived in Mrs. Sprigg's boarding house, part of Carroll Row, where the Jefferson Building now stands.

How many bricks were used to construct the Library?

There were 24 million red bricks and 550,000 enameled bricks. The enameled bricks were manufactured in Leeds, England, which created an uproar from American manufacturers, but no American contractor had put in a bid.

How much was paid for marble used to construct the Library?

Congress paid $600,000 for marble from Italy and red marble from Tunisia. It also paid $38,000 for marble from Georgia and Tennessee.

How fast were bricks laid in constructing the Library?

There were 300 men engaged to lay 50,000 bricks a day. On a good day, they laid 80,000 bricks.

What were working conditions like in constructing the Library?

It was an almost militaristic operation with little noise, except from the trowel, the hammer, the chisel, and the saw. Strict discipline was observed among the men. There were no breaks to chat, smoke, or get a drink.

How were elevators tested in the new Library building?

Engineer Green reported an air-cushion drop that included a bag full of eggs, which did not crack.

How long did it take to build the Library?

Construction took approximately seven years and was completed in 1897.

When did the Library of Congress open its doors to the public?

November 1, 1897.

Beer Bust: Shortly after the new Library of Congress Building opened in 1897, a caterer named Mills announced that he was going to sell beer at the Library. He declared he had authority from Library Superintendent Green to sell it without a license. An "indignation meeting" was held in the Foundry Methodist Church and a committee formed to stop the project. The committee went to the president who referred them to someone else. When the committee threatened to raid the bar, the caterer backed down. Mills did, however, open a "blind pig," that is, an illicit place to drink, next to his restaurant, where considerable caution was practiced so that people would not notice beer being sold. He explained to a newspaperman that he had to be very careful as the "temperance folks might catch on and raise Cain." He said that the "Prohibitionists are a nuisance, and always trying to make trouble over a little beer."

On the Sly: Another temperance organization, the American Anti-Saloon League, wrote to Librarian Young on December 30, 1897: " As you doubtless know by observation, it is as safe to trust a liquor seller to dispense only wine and beer and nothing stronger as it is to trust a viper to tickle you with its tongue and withhold its fangs."

What Library scam occurred in 1897?

A few days after the new Library Building opened, Sigmund Eisenmann of New York City wrote to Librarian Young inquiring whether two young ladies representing themselves as Library employees were genuine. The women claimed that the Library would send a set of free books to 30,000 residents of New York State. Moreover, $17 million would be distributed from Library funds to New Yorkers. To qualify, all one needed was to sign one's name in a book.

What Library scam occurred in 1935?

In 1935, certain people received letters offering to place biographies and pictures of deceased relatives in the files of the Library of Congress as a "permanent record of their achievements." The cost for this service, which included copyright, was $110, a considerable sum for Depression years when the average rent for an apartment was $30 a month. Copyrighting brief material, such as a newspaper story, cost $1 in 1935. When informed of this offer, Librarian Putnam said the Library did not "countenance" such plans.

What concessionaire request did the Library receive?

On April 30, 1898, Mr. J. A. Bower requested permission to sell opera and reading glasses inside the Library.

When was the first non-Library reception held in the new Library building?

John W. Foster (1836–1917), diplomat and former secretary of state, requested facilities for a reception given to the "Joint High Commission" composed of the United States and Great Britain to resolve Canadian border adjustments. The Joint Library Committee voted and granted permission on December 5, 1898.

What role did photography play in constructing the Library?

Time-lapse photography recorded the progress of construction every ten days on the same spot. Some 900 glass negatives of the construction's progress were made. The photographs were to settle disputes with contractors, align construction for engineers, and present a documentary record for historians.

What are the sculptures on the three bronze doors of the Jefferson Building?

The door sculptures depict three stages of the Literary Tradition: the Oral Method by which knowledge was first transmitted; Writing from the Egyptians, Hebrews, and Greeks; and the Art of Typography, with symbols of learning such as the owl, the hourglass, and the figure of Minerva, goddess of wisdom.

What are the dimensions of the doors?

The doors are 14 feet high and 7-1/2 feet wide.

How much do the doors weigh?

Together, the doors weigh 3.5 tons or 1.16 tons each.

What is the architectural style of the Jefferson Building?

The building is in the Italian Renaissance Revival style. The interior of the Great Hall with its columns, arches, and marble staircase is in the Beaux Arts style.

How many artists worked on the building?

Working to complete the Jefferson Building were twenty-two American sculptors and twenty American painters. Almost all had studied art in Europe.

What do the carved heads outside the building represent?

Thirty-three granite heads seen outside the building represent the various ethnological types of mankind. They are modeled after studies collected by the National Museum. Professor Otis T. Mason of the museum's Department of Ethnology (today the Smithsonian's Museum of Natural History) provided source materials. Each sculpture fits the allotted space. Thus, the American Indian's feathers lie flat rather than stand up.

What is unusual about some of these ethnic heads?

Some are based on contemporary figures, most notably the Semitic and Hungarian prototypes. A colorful Turkish Jew named Far-Away Moses is the model for the Semitic  head. During the nineteenth century, he was the most famous dragoman (tour guide) in Constantinople. On his 1867 voyage to Palestine, Mark Twain made his acquaintance and was said to have given him his nickname, since Moses was constantly running ahead of tourists and, when

Among the Library's ethnic heads on the Jefferson Building keystone are two standouts—Faraway Moses (middle, top), who was Mark Twain's Constantinople tour guide, and Louis C. Solyom (middle, bottom), the only staff member featured in Library decoration.

needed by Twain, was always far away. An early guidebook had, however, already mentioned Far-Away by name. To frustrate his guide, who was proud of his moniker, Twain, in fact, insisted on calling him Ferguson. The ethnic head representing a Hungarian is modeled after Louis C. Solyom, who was a foreign language cataloger for forty-six years.

Who is given preeminence among the nine busts in the portico?

Above the main entrance of the Jefferson Building are nine granite busts of famous authors. From left to right, they include: Demosthenes, Emerson, Irving, Goethe, Franklin, Macaulay, Hawthorne, Sir Walter Scott, and Dante. Each bust is three feet high, but Franklin in the center appears preeminent.

What did President Franklin D. Roosevelt propose for the Library in 1934?

FDR believed the Library's Italian Renaissance style was "out of tune" with the classical architecture of surrounding buildings. When the press got word of his proposal to remodel the dome, the plan was quickly dropped.

How many quotations line the walls of the Great Hall?

There are twenty-nine inscriptions taken from the Bible and poets ranging from Ovid to Shakespeare and Emerson.

Seeing the Light: Colonel Willard Webb of the Library staff was once asked to identify the following quotation:

> As one lamp lights
> Another nor grows less,
> So nobleness
> Enkindleth nobleness.

Though it seemed familiar, neither he nor his colleagues could track it down. The next day, he picked up a book entitled *Inscriptions* by Charles W. Eliot. On page 36, Willard Webb found the source: the quotation was inscribed in one of the panels of the Library dome above his own desk. It was suggested by President Eliot of Harvard University who had provided quotations for the Library at the request of Librarian Spofford.

What American woman poet wrote a poem about the Library?

Amy Lowell wrote "The Congressional Library."

What does the floor of the Great Hall show?

The brown and white marble floor shows a brass sunburst with points of the compass surrounded by signs of the zodiac. The marble work was done by Batterson, See, and Eisele, who had designed three Vanderbilt residences, as well as all the leading banks and insurance companies of New York City.

What feat did Library architects accomplish that will probably never be repeated?

The Library was completed under budget. Of the original $6.5 million appropriation, $213,443.40 were returned to Congress. To

When the *Literary Digest International Book Review* printed this beautiful word picture describing the Jefferson Building by poet Amy Lowell in 1922, the second and third stanzas were transposed in error.

give an idea of the magnitude of this feat, the cost of restoration of the Jefferson and Adams buildings begun in 1980 had exceeded $100 million by 1997.

What is the most beautiful room in the Library?

The Members of Congress Room is the acknowledged showpiece of the Library. Reserved for representatives and senators, it has oak-paneled walls eleven feet high, a beamed ceiling with painted panels, and marble fireplaces at either end of the room. Above one fireplace is a mosaic representing Law and over the other a mosaic depicting History.

What is the motif of the second floor corridors?

Fifty-six printer's marks in triangular borders can be seen on the walls. Traditionally, these personal emblems of fifteenth- and sixteenth-century printers were placed in colophons at the end of books and were later put on title pages.

> **Printer's Marks:** The mark of Aldus Manutius of Venice shows a dolphin and anchor. That of Melchior Sessa of Venice shows a cat, sometimes with a mouse. Christoph Froschauer of Zurich pictorialized his name, which in German means frog in a meadow. These decorative designs served as trademarks, identifying printers who took pride in their craftsmanship. Only three years after the invention of printing, the first printer's mark appeared in the 1457 Psalter published by Johann Fust and Peter Schoeffer in Mainz.

Was real gold leaf used in Library decorations?

Originally, 10,000 square feet of the dome and the flame of the Torch of Learning were finished with 23-carat gold leaf.

How much did gold leaf cost in 1893?

$27 an ounce. Gold itself cost $17 an ounce.

What was the bill for the Library's gold leaf?

The bill for gold leaf covering the dome and the flame of the Torch of Learning came to $3,800.

Are the dome and the flame still covered with gold?

Today, copper covers the dome; only the flame is golden.

How high is the Torch of Learning?

The torch is twelve feet high.

What twelve-inch object protrudes from the flame?

A lightning rod about the size of a pencil.

In the Great Hall, what do the two female statues standing at the foot of the staircase represent?

Both show Minerva, the Roman goddess of war and wisdom. One holds a sword and torch. The other holds a torch and scroll.

How many marble children are sculpted on the grand staircases?

There are a total of twenty-six children on the right and left staircases leading to the second floor.

What is the significance of these marble children?

Each child represents a profession. On the left staircase are a gardener with spade and rake; a butterfly collector with net; a scholar reading; and a printer with page proof. Further along are a musician with lyre; a doctor mixing medicine; an electrician holding a telephone; and an astronomer with telescope. On the outside of the stairs are children representing Asia and Europe separated by a globe. Above the landing are three children representing art: a painter with palette; an architect with compass and scroll; and a sculptor at work on a statue.

On the right staircase are a mechanic with cogwheel; a hunter holding gun and rabbit; a vintner with glass of champagne; a farmer with sheaf of wheat and sickle; a fisherman with rod and reel; a warrior holding a helmet; a chemist with bottle; and a cook with kettle on the fire. On the outside of the stairs are children representing Africa and America separated by a globe. Above the landing are three children representing literature: one with the mask of comedy; one with the scroll of poetry; and one with the mask of tragedy.

Who sculpted the marble children?

Philip Martiny (1858–1927). He was born in Strasbourg, France, and came to New York as a young man. He also sculpted the lions in the Boston Public Library and the bronze doors of St. Bartholomew's Church in Manhattan.

Where did Martiny find the model for his American Indian child?

He went to Buffalo Bill's Wild West Show and chose an Indian child.

How did Library sculptors achieve their intricate detail in marble?

Sculptors used a new device, the compressed air chisel, which resembled the drill used by dentists. It strikes marble 1,200 to 1,500 times a minute.

What is unusual about the baseball and football panels on the south corridor ceiling?

American athletes are completely naked in the style of Greek and Roman athletes.

What is the most beautiful gallery in the Library?

By consensus, the Library's most beautiful gallery is the Pavilion of the Discoverers located in the Southwest Pavilion. A painting by George Willoughby Maynard in the domed ceiling of this magnificent room forms a giant disc whose four female figures standing north, south, east, and west represent *Courage, Valor, Fortitude,* and *Achievement.*

Courage wears armor covered by a lion's skin and holds a shield and club.

Valor, also clad in armor, covers her heart with her left hand and holds a sword in her right.

Fortitude holds a column in her left hand and gathers her sash in her right.

Achievement holds the Roman eagle standard in her left hand and touches her throat with her right.

The four figures are symbolically linked to four wall paintings called lunettes. These lunettes have as their subjects *Adventure, Discovery, Conquest,* and *Civilization:*

Adventure holds the staff of Mercury (god of the traveler) in her left hand and a drawn sword in her right. She is flanked by two figures representing England and Spain whose civilizations produced most of the explorers.

Discovery holds a globe in her left hand and a ship's rudder in her right. She is flanked by two figures, one pointing toward the horizon with chart and paddle and the other holding a sword and navigational device.

Conquest wears a helmet pushed back and lightly grips her sword. She is flanked by two figures representing Spain's conquest of the southern hemisphere and England's of the northern.

Civilization holds the torch of learning and a book. She has donned a robe in place of armor and is flanked by Agriculture and Manufacturing.

What is the meaning of the fresco in the collar of the dome?

The fresco painted by Edwin H. Blashfield (1848–1936) is entitled, *The Evolution of Civilization.* It shows twelve figures symbolizing the nations that contributed to the advancement of world culture.

Egypt holds a tablet with hieroglyphics and the ankh of immortality. He represents the Written Record.

Judea holds her hands in prayer and wears a breastplate with the names of the Twelve Tribes. The Hebrew inscription on the pillar reads: "Thou shalt love thy neighbor as thyself."

Greece is seated by a bronze lamp symbolizing wisdom and wears the crown of Athens, the Mother of Philosophy.

Rome wears armor and a lion's skin representing the empire's public administration of Europe and Asia Minor. His foot rests on a marble column symbolizing stability.

Islam, represented by an Arab, holds a book of calculations as a tribute to the Arab genius in expanding scientific and mathematical knowledge. His foot rests on a glass retort.

The Middle Ages holds a sword and other weapons representing chivalry. She rests her elbow on a miniature gothic cathedral. The papal tiara and keys of St. Peter symbolize the power of the Church.

Italy holds a palette and paintbrush representing the flowering of Renaissance art. To her left is a replica of Michelangelo's *David*. Against her foot is a Stradivarius violin. She has the likeness of Amy Rose, woman sculptress from New York.

Germany is a printer examining sheets just off the printing press. The model was General Thomas Lincoln Casey, the Library's architect.

Spain represents the Age of Exploration and holds the tiller of a caravel. He is based on Blashfield's sketch of the painter William Bailey Faxon.

England symbolizes the Golden Age of Literature and has a book on her lap that shows the original title page of *A Midsummer Night's Dream*. She has the likeness of nineteenth-century English actress Ellen Terry.

France represents Emancipation and wears a liberty cap with tricolor cockade. In her hand, she holds the Declaration of the Rights of Man. The model for France is the artist's wife.

America symbolizes genius in the mechanical and engineering arts. The features of the contemplative worker-scientist are said to have been modeled after young Abraham Lincoln.

Artist Edwin H. Blashfield surveys the sweep of civilization in his mural under the dome of the Library's Main Reading Room.

How tall are the twelve figures in the dome?

They appear of no great height but are really ten feet tall.

Why does each figure have wings in the background?

Wings heighten the sense that each figure stands for the ascent of civilization. Overlapping wings unite the entire composition.

How did Blashfield change his original fresco design?

He originally proposed to set Byzantium between Rome and Italy to represent the Codification of Law. He decided instead to depict an Arab representing the transmission of science and mathematics to Europe. He also planned for Germany to represent the Reformation but instead had it represent the Invention of Printing.

How did he paint the fresco?

He used a revolving trolley with a scaffold designed by Bernard R. Green to navigate the great room. The vehicle enabled Blashfield and his assistant, Arthur R. Willett, to reach the Rotunda's dome collar. Unlike Michelangelo who painted the Sistine Chapel on his back, Blashfield reclined in a beach chair.

How did a schoolmate describe him?

A reminiscence by schoolmate Royal Cortissoz shows the esteem he held for Blashfield: "There was something symbolical in two words that he spoke to me once, years ago. He was painting the decoration in the dome at the Congressional Library and I had an appointment there to meet him and watch him work. I stood at the foot of the interminable flimsy staircase that led to the scaffolding at the top and called. Blashfield leaned over and cried, "Come up!" It might have been his watchword. All his life, in his character, in his work, in every phase of his career, he summoned his fellows to a higher plane."

How much did Blashfield earn for his fresco?

$10,000.

How large was his estate?

Not exactly the starving artist, Blashfield died at the height of the Depression and left an estate valued at $1,023,421, of which $1 million were in securities.

Who selected the historical figures for the Reading Room's portrait statues?

Librarian Spofford selected the figures from Moses to Joseph Henry.

Who selected the sculptors for the Reading Room's statues?

A committee of three sculptors, Augustus Saint-Gaudens, John Quincy Adams Ward, and Olin Levi Warner, selected them.

How tall are the bronze statues in the Main Reading Room?

Almost seven feet tall. The statue of Michelangelo is taller than the rest and is considered the best sculpture.

What do the bronze statues overlooking the Main Reading Room represent?

Moses with the tablets of the law and St. Paul with sword and scroll represent religion.

Columbus and Robert Fulton holding a model of the *Clermont,* the first steamboat, represent commerce.

Herodotus, Greek historian, called father of history, and Gibbon, author of *The Decline and Fall of the Roman Empire,* represent history.

Michelangelo, whose statue is larger than the others, and Beethoven, who cups his ear to hear better, represent the arts.

Plato and Francis Bacon represent philosophy.

Homer and Shakespeare represent poetry.

Solon, the Athenian, with his scroll of "The Laws" and Chancellor James Kent of New York with his *Commentaries on American Law* represent law.

Newton and Joseph Henry, physicist and first secretary of the Smithsonian Institution holding an electromagnet, represent science.

Viewed above Michelangelo and going clockwise are eight plaster figures eleven feet high representing various aspects of civilization:

Art (after a plan by Augustus Saint-Gaudens) holds a model of the Parthenon in Athens.

History (by Daniel Chester French) holds a mirror to look backward in time.

The greatest of all sculptors is seen here as a sculpture himself in Paul Bartlett's plaster model for the bronze Michelangelo in the Main Reading Room.

Commerce (by John F. Flanagan) holds a Yankee schooner and locomotive.

Law (by Paul W. Bartlett) holds a scroll and Tablet of the Law.

Religion (by Theodore Baur) holds a flower.

Science (by John Donoghue) holds a globe in her left hand and a mirror turned outward in her right.

Poetry (by John Quincy Adams Ward) wears a symbolic robe suggesting lines of verse.

Philosophy (by Bela L. Pratt) holds a book.

What is seen in the lantern of the dome?

There is the painting of a woman representing *Human Understanding* lifting the veil of human knowledge. She looks from the finite human achievement indicated by the fresco toward infinity above. She is attended by two cherubs, one of whom holds a closed book.

What is the meaning of the mosaic at the top of the staircase leading to the Visitors' Gallery?

It shows the third representation of Minerva in the Great Hall. As the guardian of the Main Reading Room, she has placed her shield and helmet at her feet and holds her spear in readiness. In her left hand is a scroll listing various academic disciplines. She is flanked by a statue of Victory and an owl. Beneath her is a Latin inscription from Horace's *Ars poetica:*

"Nil invita Minerva, quae monumentum aere perennius exegit"
(Willingly, Minerva raises a monument more lasting than bronze).

What is curious about Minerva's toes?

Whether seen from the right, center, or left, Minerva's toes appear to point toward the viewer.

No Exceptions: Six tiles from Minerva's robe were missing. An order was issued to Library police that visitors must check their umbrellas and canes because tourists used them to point out the intricate tile work in the Minerva mosaic. Shortly thereafter, the guard on duty saw a party of gentlemen approaching carrying canes and top hats. The guard asked them to check their canes. One man questioned the guard if this was necessary. It was the president's secretary; standing behind him was Woodrow Wilson. Before the guard could reply, the president spoke up: "Why not? It's the rule of the institution. I'm checking my cane—come on, you may as well check yours, too."

What is the significance of the seals on the windows of the Main Reading Room?

Different types of translucent glass were used to lessen the effect of direct sunlight on the eight semicircular windows with their stained glass seals and on the readers below. Above each window is the American eagle and below it the Great Seal of the United States. To the right and left are the state seals beginning with the thirteen original states. Only states and territories up to 1897 are represented. The final three seals are of New Mexico, Arizona, and Oklahoma, which were still territories in 1897.

What Library decoration took the longest to put in place?

The clock designed in marble and bronze by John F. Flanagan for the Main Reading Room was five years late in arriving. Even then, there were difficulties with the serpentine hands, which were too heavy for the clock's mechanism.

What is the clock's motif?

Above the clock, Father Time stands with a scythe. Flanking him are figures representing the seasons. The clock's dial is four feet in diameter, the hands set with semiprecious stones. The clock is directly below the Visitors' Gallery of the Main Reading Room.

What design by the clock's sculptor do all Americans carry in their pockets?

John F. Flanagan designed the George Washington 25-cent coin.

What American artist residing in London declined to contribute his work to the Jefferson Building?

John Singer Sargent.

Why were the Library's architecture and art work such spectacular successes?

They were planned by few people. No large committees were involved.

> **Book Spiral:** In 1872, Librarian Spofford predicted 2,500,000 books would be in the collections by the year 1972. The actual figure was more than six times that amount. General Casey, the Library architect, estimated in 1907 that at the annual rate of accession of 30,000 volumes, there would be enough book space in the Jefferson Building for ninety-eight years. By 1935, the rate of accession was over 186,000 volumes and a year later more than 228,000

What was accomplished in the renovation of the Jefferson Building begun in 1980?

Art works were restored and more than 100 murals cleaned. Gilded areas throughout the building were restored.

A Wilton carpet was purchased for the Main Reading Room; it has a motif of rosettes and wreaths patterned after the room's architecture; the carpet's open book design reflects the thousands of books in the alcoves.

The massive card catalog was removed from the Main Reading Room to add forty-four new desks, for a total of 226 with outlets for laptop computers.

Telecommunication cables were installed throughout the building.

More than one hundred miles of fiber-optic cables were added to the Main Reading Room and the adjacent Computer Catalog Center.

Fire alarm and sprinkler systems were modernized.

The Jefferson Building roof and dome were repaired.

The Coolidge Auditorium was renovated.

> **Cover-up:** Sprinkler heads were installed in the classical rosettes found in the ceilings of the Main Reading Room and the exhibition galleries. The sprinklers are so well hidden and integrated that casual observers cannot see them.

What did critics say when the Jefferson Building reopened?

The building was called "a Fabergé egg with wonders inside" and "the First National Bank of American Creativity."

THE JOHN ADAMS BUILDING

Why was the Annex (now called the John Adams Building) constructed?

It was intended as a book stack.

When did the building open?

January 3, 1939.

Who were the architects?

The architectural firm of Pierson and Wilson. Alexander Buel Trowbridge was the consulting architect.

How much did the building cost?

$8.2 million.

How large is the building?

Built in the Art Deco style, the Adams Building has 249 miles of shelving. It houses most of the Library's book collections. There are twelve tiers of book stacks capable of accommodating ten million volumes.

What are on the building's bronze doors?

Twelve figures representing ancient civilizations.

What are the motifs connecting these civilizations?

The motifs connecting them are the graphic arts, learning, and writing.

Who represents each civilization?

The figures present graphic arts to their people:

Thoth to Egypt.	*Hermes to the Greeks.*
Ts'ang Chieh to China.	*Odin to the Norse.*
Nabu to Sumer and Akkad.	*Ogma to the Irish.*
Brahma to India.	*Itzama to the Mayas.*
Cadmus to Greece.	*Quetzalcoatl to the Aztecs.*
Tahmurath to Persia.	*Sequoyah to the Cherokees.*

Where can you see the pilgrims from Chaucer's **Canterbury Tales?**

In murals in the North Reading Room of the Adams Building. The reading room is on the fifth floor and provides facilities for readers of business and economics, and science and technology.

Who painted the **Canterbury Tales** *murals?*

Artist Ezra Winter from Traverse City, Michigan.

What is unique about them?

They are painted on canvas and show Chaucer himself among thirty-two pilgrims. Chaucer rides a black horse between the Doctor of Physic and the Lawyer.

Where can you see the Jefferson murals?

In the South Reading Room of the Adams Building.

Who painted the Jefferson murals?

They are also the work of Ezra Winter.

What are the motifs connecting these murals?

The motifs connecting them are the basic ideas of the Jeffersonian Creed: man as guardian of his own freedom; the goodness of the earth; the dignity of labor and the virtues of agrarian life; and public education. Students at the University of Virginia are contrasted with figures representing greed and superstition and the pagan temple of Stonehenge.

Who once lived on the site of the Adams Building?

Lincoln's secretary, John Nicolay.

What was placed on the roof of the Adams Building during World War II?

Anti-aircraft gun batteries were installed. The Library provided quarters in Attic Room B where the gun crews could rest.

THE JAMES MADISON
MEMORIAL BUILDING

When was the Madison Building constructed?

Between 1974 and 1981.

Who were the architects?

The architectural firm of DeWitt, Poor, and Shelton.

How large is the building?

The largest office building on Capitol Hill, the Madison Building has more floor space than any federal building in the Washington area except for the Pentagon and the Hoover FBI Building.

What special features does it have?

The Madison Building has motorized book stacks for the Music Division and the Law Library. In addition, the building can accommodate fifty million items in special format, such as sound recordings, prints and photographs, maps, music manuscripts, and presidential papers and other manuscripts.

How much did the building cost?

$120 million.

Why were Madison Building architects limited to six stories?

No building on Capitol Hill may be higher than the Capitol.

Why could the Madison Building cellar not be built deeper?

The Tiber Creek runs beneath the building.

B O O K S

When did the Library publish its first catalog?

In 1802, the first *Catalogue of the Books, Maps, and Charts Belonging to the Library of the Two Houses of Congress* listed 964 volumes.

How many German books did the Library own?

When Alois Freiherr von Lederer, consul general of Austro-Hungary in New York, visited the Library around 1820, he noted that he could not locate even one German book although Germans constituted the second largest immigrant group.

How does the Library get most of its books?

Through copyright and purchase. Under copyright law, the Library receives two copies of each book published in the United States. Originally, the Smithsonian Institution and the Library of Congress received one copy of each book published in the United States. In 1870, legislation gave the Library sole authority to copyright books, photographs, maps, and music produced in this country. In 1891, international copyright agreements increased the Library's collections with the deposit of foreign books.

Where does the Library keep books?

The Jefferson Building contains nine separate levels of book stacks in the southeast portion of the building and nine in the northwest, all of them accessible by elevator or stairs. The book stacks begin in the basement of the building and rise sixty-three feet. Each tier or stack is seven feet in height and separated from those above and below by iron floors. The public may not enter the book stacks.

What does the Library do with unwanted books?

Most books not selected for the collections are offered to American and foreign institutions on an exchange and gift basis.

What did the Library acquire from the Smithsonian Institution?

In 1866, the Smithsonian Institution library was transferred to the Library of Congress. These 40,000 volumes gave the Library the most extensive collection of scientific books and journals in the nation.

Which 1876 congressional resolution brought a flood of books to the Library?

Congress requested each community in the Union to write the history of its locality and send a copy to the Library. These publications became known as "mug books" because of the portraits of people from the various communities.

How fast did the Library's classification system grow?

In 1897, the scheme for the classification of books in the Library could fit on one page. By 1938, it took 5,720 pages in 25 separate volumes. By 1997, the number of pages to cover classification tables had exceeded 14,000 pages.

How fast did the Library's list of Subject Headings grow?

In 1919, the Library's list of *Subject Headings* amounted to 1,315 pages in one volume. In 1999, it totalled 6,526 pages in five volumes.

AWOL: After ninety years' absence, an edition of Virgil's works was returned to the Library in 1950. It was found among the papers of John C. Breckenridge, member of Congress, vice president of the United States, Senator, and major general in the Confederate Army. The book had to be reclassified since it had been shelved according to the original Jeffersonian system.

What did the emperor of China give to the Library?

In 1869, the emperor gave the Library almost 1,000 volumes, thus laying the foundation for the Chinese collection.

What books does the Library collect that measure 3-1/2" x 17-1/2"?

Tibetan religious texts between wooden board covers.

Perilous Journey: Obtaining books for the Library sometimes takes more than just ordering from a book dealer.

In 1925, Dr. Joseph F. Rock, botanist at the Department of Agriculture and explorer for the *National Geographic,* sought refuge from brigands at the great Lamaist monastery in Choni on the Chinese-Tibetan frontier. There, he discovered a trove of books much wanted by the Library of Congress. They comprised a complete set of Tibetan Buddhist religious rules printed from five-hundred-year-old woodblocks.

In all, there were 317 volumes, each consisting of several hundred leaves of eight thin pages pasted together. The pages were nearly two feet long and from six to eight inches wide. For protection, Dr. Rock packed them in wooden boxes, each holding three or four volumes. In all, ninety-two wooden boxes were needed. The boards for the boxes had to be sawed from fourteen logs. Because there was no oiled packing paper available, Dr. Rock had to round up beeswax to seal the boxes.

The nearest railroad was thirty days from Choni. Mules had to be secured from another city. The caravan started from Choni on February 26, 1926. When it arrived at a Chinese post office, the boxes were found to be overweight but were sent after paying a registered mail fee of $530.20 in Mexican currency. After eighteen days, the boxes reached Sian Fu, capital of Shensi Province. Because the city was under siege, the boxes remained at the post office for more than six months. During this time, the postmaster was shot and the registered mail looted by bandits. Fortunately, Tibetan texts did not interest the robbers.

In May 1927, the books finally reached Shanghai where they were bound into volumes Tibetan style with wooden slabs as covers to make them into a volume. In July 1928, after nearly two and a half years, the books finally arrived in Washington. The Choni books are the only copies in the West. The Lamaist monastery was destroyed by fire shortly after the books came to the Library of Congress.

What is the largest encyclopedia in the Library?

A Chinese encyclopedia entitled *T'u shu chi ch'eng* contains more than ten thousand books bound in 5,040 volumes. Compiled by order of Manchu Emperor K'ang Hsi and published in 1726, it was a gift to the United States for cancelling indemnities incurred during the Boxer Rebellion.

The Library owns the world's largest encyclopedia. Completed in 1726 for a Manchu emperor, it consists of 5,040 volumes.

How long does it take for a book to be cataloged and reach the shelf for readers?

On average, two months. It depends on the difficulty of the book or whether it deals with a subject new to the Library's list of approved subject headings. Often, a book of less than a hundred pages is more difficult to catalog than one of five hundred pages, the reason being that the smaller book will deal with a very specific and unknown subject.

When did the Library first use catalog cards?

Although Harvard University had adopted a card catalog in 1856, a drawer with catalog cards was not to be found at the Library of Congress until 1881. Before then, catalogs were printed in bound volumes too cumbersome to use. The first catalog cards were pieces of paper measuring 17-7/10 x 11-2/5 cm. clipped from the printed catalog. The now-familiar standard-size cards, 7-1/2 x 12-1/2 cm. were not used until 1897.

What used to be a Library staff member's nightmare?

Dropping a tray of catalog cards was much dreaded. The tray had to be left where it fell so that an expert filer could rearrange the cards.

When did the Card Distribution Service begin?

The Card Distribution Service began on April 5, 1899. The cost of cataloging a book and printing a card was thirty cents. From 1901 to 1976, about 1,613,111,283 cards representing 6 million titles were sold. At its peak in 1968, orders for cards were 60,000 a day. But then, automation began. Gradually, computers and optical readers began to replace staff. After 1997, no more cards were printed.

How many people worked in Card Distribution?

The staff required for printing, distributing, and searching catalog cards amounted to twenty percent of total Library staff or 564 people. They worked in two shifts. Fifty special stools with oversize casters were needed so that searchers could quickly move from one alphabet to another.

Not even the Library of Alexandria, wonder of the ancient world, could equal this tower of Library catalog cards (1917).

How much does the Library save other libraries each year?

By cataloging some 300,000 books and journals each year, the Library saves American libraries about $268 million.

How many items does the Library acquire each day?

About 22,000 items. These include books, recordings, copyright deposits, and maps.

When was the last catalog card printed at the Library?

The last catalog card (for Clark G. Reynolds' *War in the Pacific*) was produced in May 1997.

Everyone knows about the Year 2000 problem. What was the Library's 1998 problem?

Books assigned the Library's catalog number beginning with 98- were in conflict with catalog cards printed in 1898. The problem was resolved by not reusing the numbers assigned in 1898.

How many items does the Library own?

As of 2000, about 119 million items. These include books, films, maps, manuscripts, prints, and photographs.

Who may borrow books from the Library?

Members of Congress have priority in borrowing books. Others with borrowing privileges are Library staff, government officials, government libraries, and foreign ambassadors. Loans are also made to research libraries through interlibrary loan, which began in 1907.

What notable book did President Lincoln borrow in 1861?

A Key to Uncle Tom's Cabin by Harriet Beecher Stowe.

Which books cannot be borrowed?

Rare books, books on local U.S. history, and books on genealogy.

Whose family tree is on display at the Library?

The Local History and Genealogy Reading Room displays George Washington's pedigree panel. The pedigree is executed in brilliant colors on a panel seven feet high and ten feet long. The Washington family is traced from King John who signed the Magna Carta in 1215 and from nine barons. The panel was a gift of the British Government to the Library.

How can the Library produce a cataloging record before a book is even published?

Since 1971, American publishers inform the Library of future publications. Library catalogers prepare records (often from sparse information) and assign a classification number which is then printed on the verso of each book's title page. This joint Library-publisher program is known as CIP (Cataloging in Publication).

For whom does the Library summarize the contents of a book in one sentence?

Since 1965, cataloging records of books for young readers have been annotated with "a short, concise summary, not critical or evaluative in any way." All such catalog records have the phrase "Juvenile literature" added.

What is the purpose of the Library's overseas offices?

Since 1962, the Library has maintained field offices in Rio de Janeiro, Brazil; Cairo, Egypt; New Delhi, India; Jakarta, Indonesia; Nairobi, Kenya; and Karachi, Pakistan. There is also an acquisitions office in Moscow.

These Library outposts serve more than sixty countries in collecting publications that are difficult to obtain through other channels. They also use local staff with language expertise to catalog books and other Library material. Cataloging records from overseas are transmitted electronically to Washington.

In how many languages are books cataloged?

Books in 470 languages are represented. Library staff have expertise in sixty-three spoken languages.

What will happen when the Library runs out of space?

Anticipating this scenario, the Library is constructing storage sites at Fort Meade, Maryland.

How large is the Library's Culpeper storage site?

In 1997, the Library obtained a 140,000-square-foot storage site near Culpeper,

Virginia, about seventy miles southwest of Washington. Carved into a mountainside in the 1960's, the site was originally intended to house bank officials and to store currency and bullion in case of nuclear war. The Culpeper site, to be known as the National Audiovisual Conservation Center, will store a large part of the Library's enormous collection of films, including 500,000 cans of safety film, 110,000 cans of older film, 85,000 television programs, and 2.5 million sound recordings. The Library's Motion Picture, Broadcasting and Recorded Sound Division will also be located at this facility. Researchers on Capitol Hill and elsewhere will access films through fiber-optic cables from Culpeper.

How can non-profit organizations obtain free surplus books from the Library of Congress?

Non-profit organizations must designate a non-Library representative to select books at the Library. For further information, write to the Library of Congress Exchange and Gift Division (LM-B03), Washington D.C. 20540.

Does the Library collect comic books?

It certainly does. While others libraries consider them "trash," the Library of Congress realized their collectible value early.

How large is the Library's comic book collection?

It is the largest in the world. There are over 100,000 issues divided among 5,000 titles. Many are from the golden age of comics beginning in the 1930's. New issues and titles are added monthly.

Who has access to the Library's comic book collection?

Researchers only. Comic books, which are extremely fragile and deteriorate quickly, need to be protected.

WHAT THE LIBRARY
COULDN'T GET

What American treasure did the Library lose to a private collector?

On January 24, 1850, Congress debated whether to purchase Washington's "Farewell Address" for the Library. One lawmaker rose to say: "What is there so sacred in the manuscript of this address? It is known to have been the joint production of Washington and one, at least, of his Cabinet—not the emanation of his mind alone. I feel no such respect as here has been expressed for it, and cannot see how this manuscript is to effect such happy results. Anyone can have a printed copy, and read it, who desires. There is nothing to be gained by the purchase of this manuscript any more than there would be in the purchase of a walking stick which Washington used."

The final vote to purchase the document was approved on February 12, 1850, provided the purchase could "be effected on fair and just terms." The legislators had a $1,000 limit in mind. That same day, the "Farewell Address" was sold to James Lenox of New York for $2,300 and later ended up at the New York Public Library.

What European collection did the Library lose by one vote?

In 1836, the Senate debated purchasing for $50,000 the library of Count Dimitri Petrovich Buturlin, a native of Russia who died in Florence, Italy, in 1829. His collection of 25,000 volumes consisted chiefly of Greek, Latin, and Italian works published by the finest European printers, plus 240 manuscripts. The collection was offered at a knockdown price (Buturlin had paid $250,000 for it). This time, Daniel Webster, now a senator, who had voted against purchasing Jefferson's library in 1815 was all for the Buturlin purchase. The vote fell one short and the collection was lost to the Library.

What early Americana did the Library pass up?

In 1845, Obadiah Rich, U.S. consul in Valencia, Spain, offered to sell twenty-four volumes of unpublished manuscripts relating to the earliest history of America for 240 pounds, but the Library Committee refused. The collection went instead to James Lenox.

What art classic did the Library decline?

On April 6, 1854, Lucy Audubon, widow of John James Audubon, offered to sell the Library the original drawings of *Birds of America*. The Joint Committee on the Library declined her offer. Nevertheless, the library now owns two copies of Audobon's published masterpiece.

How long did it take Audubon to complete this work?

Eleven years (from 1827 to 1838). The publisher delivered the 435 hand-colored aquatinted plates to subscribers five at a time. They were produced in London and Edinburgh and cost $1,000 a set. This explains why subscribers included such names as Charles X of France; Queen Adelaide of Britain, consort of William IV; and Earl Spencer, forebear of Diana, Princess of Wales. American subscribers included Henry Clay and Daniel Webster. Complete copies rarely appear at auction now. In April 2000, a complete copy sold for $8.8 million.

What Vermont papers did the Library not purchase?

Henry Stevens of Vermont proposed to sell the Library the Journals of the General Assembly of Vermont, the laws of Vermont from 1779 to 1860, and 500 volumes of Vermont newspapers published since 1783. The Library Committee refused the offer.

What music collections could the Library not obtain?

Calling it a "melancholy admission," Carl Engel of the Library's Music Division regretted lack of funds to purchase the greatest collection of unpublished Wagneriana, offered at bargain prices. Another source offered to sell the most extensive collection of privately owned Bach manuscripts, including the *Clavierbüchlein* that J. S. Bach wrote for his son Friedemann, containing first drafts of some of the 48 preludes and fugues. Also offered to the Library were manuscripts by Haydn, Mozart, Weber, and Brahms. Unfortunately, the year was 1932, the United States was in economic depression, and funds were not available.

Who was the first reader to request a book from the Main Reading Room when it opened on November 1, 1897?

Max West, an employee of the Department of Agriculture.

What was the first book requested when the Library opened?

Roger Williams's *Year Book*. It was not on the shelf because it had just been published. Martha J. Lamb's *History of New York* was the first book lent to a reader.

What was Library Order Number 1 when the new building opened?

The order instructed heads of departments to rate staff and assign points for quality of work, efficiency, punctuality, and good conduct. Promotion depended on meeting or exceeding standards.

What foreign manual became the basis for many rules and regulations governing the new Library?

A Handbook for Readers at the British Museum by Thomas Nichols (1866) spelled out regulations for copying from books and manuscripts, explained arrangement of collections in reading rooms, and provided guides to catalogs. Readers could be excluded for "annoying lady-readers [and] insulting the officials." What distinguished the Library of Congress from the British Museum and most European libraries was the fact that readers did not have to present a letter of introduction or recommendation.

When did the Library first open on Sunday?

September 14, 1902. Attendance by researchers exceeded all expectations. On average, 551 people came on Sunday compared to 439 on weekdays.

How many reading rooms does the Library have?

There are twenty reading rooms.

How fast was book-paging service in 1900?

Library staff prided themselves on quick response to reader requests. During an international conference of geographers, a test was held in the Map Division to determine how long it would take to retrieve an 1874 map of Missouri. The map was handed to the requester in ninety seconds. The conference burst into applause. The same requester asked for a book from the Main Reading Room. The book arrived in three-and-a-half minutes. The reading room cheered.

Who can use Library reading rooms?

Any adult. However, high school students and younger children are not admitted. Researchers need an I.D. but it is not necessary to be a U.S. citizen.

Class Act: A school teacher presented herself to the guard at the door of the Main Reading Room on April 24, 1950 with seventy junior high school students. The guard explained that sightseers should see the room from the Gallery.

The teacher then stated that each of the children had a project to look up in the public catalog. The guard explained that children under sixteen were not admitted to the Reading Room unless accompanied by an adult. "Yes, I called the Library and was so informed," the teacher replied. "I am the adult."

Who went game-hunting in the Library?

In its August 1, 1904 issue, The *Washington Star* reported that the Library had engaged J. Eakin Gadsby, an expert marksman, to rid the Main Reading Room of pigeons that had entered the dome through ventilators. Aiming at the birds was extremely difficult and time-consuming because the marksman did not want to

This 1965 shot of the Main Reading Room being renovated looks like a Gothic cathedral under construction.

strike statues or costly decorations with his air rifle. Gadsby bagged three birds. In the first fifty years of the Main Reading Room, Library maintenance staff also hunted bats and pigeons with nets.

Out of Pocket: Before the Depression, 250 people a day were considered a record crowd for the Main Reading Room. In 1933, an average of 1,500 people a day used the Main Reading Room. What did they research? Most came to read on finance and economics.

Even the Library of Congress engaged in what it called "depression bartering" when its Map Division exchanged five triplicate maps for a 1903 atlas of Sebastian County, Arkansas, from a dealer at Fort Smith, Arkansas.

Who started recycling at the Library?

Because of reader demand for pencils, Colonel Webb of the Main Reading Room asked staff in 1954 to cut pencils in half. "If other divisions would send to the Stack and Reader Division pencils that have become too short for normal use, they can still be used by readers."

How many books are contained in the Main Reading Room reference collection?

There are 80,000 volumes consisting of encyclopedias, dictionaries, almanacs, yearbooks, bibliographies, and other reference works.

Nothing like Library ingenuity! When dust was flying during 1965 renovations in the Main Reading Room, they put up a parachute to catch it.

How many cards were in the Main Reading Room's catalog?

Some 25 million cards were filed in wooden cabinets. After the cards had been converted to computer records in the 1980's, the cabinets were removed and the freed space used for additional readers' desks.

Is there a fee to use Library reading rooms?

No. All services are free, except photocopying.

Which reading rooms are restricted?

Both the Jefferson Congressional Reading Room and the LaFollette Congressional Reading Room are reserved for members of Congress and their staffs.

THE   MANUSCRIPT   DIVISION

What is the size of the manuscript collections?

The Manuscript Division has over 12,000 different collections, totaling some 53 million items.

Could someone do research for you if you were unable to come to the Library?

The Manuscript Reading Room maintains a list of private researchers who have no official affiliation with the Library. The cost has to be negotiated with the researcher.

What is the rarest manuscript in the Library?

Lincoln's Gettysburg Address. The Library owns two copies, one of which is believed to be the one Lincoln read at Gettysburg.

Why do psychiatrists and students visit the Manuscript Reading Room?

They come to study the 80,000 manuscript pieces and other materials belonging to Sigmund Freud. His daughter Anna gave all his papers, as well as her own, to the Library.

What was found in the Carl Koller Collection?

In 1998, a researcher found a small packet of cocaine tucked inside an envelope. On the envelope was a prescription in Koller's handwriting. Also on the envelope was writing believed to be that of Sigmund Freud. Carl Koller was a Viennese physician who often worked with Freud. Both experimented with cocaine as an anesthetic. Koller was credited for pioneering its use in eye surgery.

What other outstanding collections are available from the Manuscript Reading Room?

Manuscripts include 130,000 items from the Alexander Graham Bell collection, including notebooks describing the first telephone call; the Wright brothers' papers with step-by-step accounts of experiments leading to the first powered flight; papers of Generals Pershing and Patton; papers of Lillian Gish and Claire Boothe Luce; and many others.

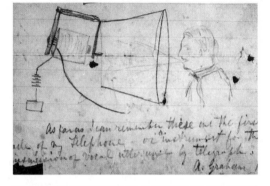

This scrap of paper from the Alexander Graham Bell Collection shows the very first sketch of what became the telephone.

How many presidential collections does the Manuscript Division own?

The papers of twenty-three presidents from Washington to Coolidge.

How extensive is the George Washington Collection?

It contains about 77,000 items on 124 reels of microfilm. About 25,000 items alone deal with his role as Commander-in-Chief of the Continental Army. Many of these are now online.

What is missing from the George Washington Collection?

First Lady Martha Washington burned all but two letters of correspondence from her husband.

What letter to the Library would make collectors weep today?

A letter written on March 15, 1899 by W. H. Snowden, historian of colonial Virginia and New Jersey, informed Assistant Librarian Spofford that a junk shop in Alexandria, Virginia, had a pile of pre-Revolutionary manuscripts weighing about 1,300 pounds on sale for half a cent a pound. No action was taken.

What happened to some of Benjamin Franklin's papers before they came to the Library?

In 1882, the American government purchased a portion of Franklin's papers from Henry Stevens, an American book dealer who lived in London. Stevens had obtained them from the estate of William Temple Franklin, Ben's grandson, who had moved to London where he lived above his landlord's tailor shop. After William Temple Franklin's death, the papers were bundled and thrown aside. Some of the papers ended up in the tailor's shop for scissoring patterns. By good fortune, the bulk of the papers were discovered by Mr. Stevens.

Whose wedding cake is preserved in a specially constructed box in the Manuscript Reading Room?

Two performers from P. T. Barnum's Museum were married in a New York ceremony attended by the Astors and Vanderbilts. They were Charles Sherwood Stratton, better known as General Tom Thumb, and Mercy Lavinia Magri. Both were under three feet in height. On their honeymoon in Washington, they were received by President and Mrs. Lincoln.

How extensive is the Abraham Lincoln Collection?

It contains about 43,000 items on ninety-six reels of microfilm.

How did the Library obtain two copies of the Gettysburg Address?

They were given to the Library in 1916 by the heirs of John Hay, Lincoln's secretary.

Who gave Lincoln's papers to the Library?

In 1923, Robert Todd Lincoln gave his father's correspondence to the American people by donating them to the Library with the stipulation that they not be made public until twenty-one years after his own death. The papers were opened one minute after midnight on July 26, 1947. Ceremonies were broadcast on international radio. The horde of researchers, members of the press, and the curious who had gathered were, in the words of the Library's Lincoln expert, "reminiscent of a national encampment of the Grand Army of the Republic."

Who was chosen to open the Lincoln documents?

The Chief Page Boy in the House of Representatives, Dorsey Joseph Bartlett, twenty years old, expressed the wish to open the papers since he was a Lincoln admirer. A Marine Corps veteran of World War II, Dorsey approached David C. Mearns, Head of the Library's Reference Department, and was surprised when his admittedly "absurd request" was granted.

Who else was present at the opening of the Lincoln documents?

Major General Ulysses S. Grant III, grandson of Lincoln's commander; Ralph G. Newman, owner of the Abraham Lincoln Book Shop in Chicago; Lincoln biographer Carl Sandburg; and Alfred Whital Stern, owner of the greatest private collection of Lincoln manuscripts and books.

Among the Library's Lincoln papers is the First Inaugural Address printed by the Illinois State Journal press before the swearing-in and showing hand corrections made by the president-elect.

What is the only book Lincoln ever edited?

Political Debates Between Hon. Abraham Lincoln and Hon. Stephen A. Douglas in the Celebrated Campaign of 1858, in Illinois. Senatorial candidate Lincoln pasted newspaper clippings in a scrapbook, edited the misquotes by hand, and let his secretary add text. The book was published to launch his presidency in 1860 and became a best seller. The Manuscript Reading Room owns the original.

How did the Library obtain Lincoln's inkstand?

It was donated to the Library in 1937 by Mrs. Charles Isham, granddaughter of the president. Originally, it had been presented to the president in 1865 by Charles D. Poston of Arizona. The stand shows "Liberty" standing on a dome similar to that of the U.S. Capitol. The silver Tiffany inkwell is flanked by two seated figures: an Indian with a hatchet and a frontiersman with a rifle.

How did the Library acquire the papers of President Chester A. Arthur?

The president's grandson Alan, also known as "Gavin," sold some of the presidential and family papers to the Library and donated the rest. Gavin led an unsettled life. He lived in a commune, sold newspapers on San Francisco streets, and dabbled in astrology and sexology. He styled himself a "pre-hippie hippie." President Arthur's papers were much sought after, because he destroyed most of them shortly before his death in 1886.

What other president destroyed all his personal papers?

Calvin Coolidge. He remarked: "I have never been hurt by what I have not said." The Library, however, owns all his official papers.

How did the Declaration of Independence and the Constitution get to the Library?

In 1921, President Harding issued an executive order transferring them from the Department of State to the Library of Congress.

Where were they kept for three years?

In Librarian Putnam's safe.

The Library houses presidential papers from Washington to Coolidge. Among the rarest are those of Chester A. Arthur, shown here in white hat with New York merchant R.G. Dun (of Bradstreet fame). Arthur's hippie grandson gathered the few letters that survived and brought them to the Library.

Where and when were they finally displayed?

On the second floor of the Great Hall from 1924 to 1952. They were housed in a specially designed marble and bronze shrine. The opening ceremony was attended by President and Mrs. Coolidge.

Why was the Declaration of Independence so poorly preserved?

In 1823, copies of the document were made for the heirs of each of the signers. The copying was done with a damp linen cloth by going over each letter with a stylus, then transferring it to a copper sheet. The copies were perfect but the process destroyed the original. From 1841 until 1877, the Declaration was kept at the Patent Office, which was then a bureau of the Department of State. While at the Patent Office, the document was positioned in such a way that, at a certain hour, a beam of sunlight would highlight the middle part of the text. This caused the ink to fade and, as a result, most of the signatures have disappeared.

Why were the Declaration of Independence and the Constitution sent to Fort Knox?

For safekeeping during World War II. They were sent on December 23, 1941, and returned to the Library on October 1, 1944. In 1952, both documents were moved to a specially built case at the National Archives where they have remained ever since.

What other Library "Top Treasures" were sent to Fort Knox?

The Gutenberg Bible, the Articles of Confederation, and the Gettysburg Address also stayed out the war at the Bullion Depository of Fort Knox, Kentucky.

How long are the Articles of Confederation?

They are on a scroll thirteen feet long.

Who was the last president to place his hand on the United States Constitution at the Library?

At a Library of Congress ceremony on Constitution Day, September 17, 1951, the Constitution was sealed in an airtight glass and metal-frame container. Before it was sealed, oxygen was removed and replaced with helium, an inert gas. The last person to touch the document was President Truman.

What is the rarest Jefferson document in the Library?

The Library owns a manuscript penned by Thomas Jefferson and known as the Rough Draft of the Declaration of Independence. It contains a total of eighty-six hand corrections, sixteen made by John Adams and Benjamin Franklin, the rest by members of the Continental Congress.

A Marine Corps tank escorts the Declaration of Independence and the Constitution to their new home at the National Archives after more than twenty years on display at the Library.

What are the Dunlap broadsides?

They are the twenty-four surviving copies of the first printing of the Declaration of Independence published by John Dunlap of Philadelphia on the evening of July 4, 1776.

The Library owns two copies, one of which is George Washington's personal copy sent to him by John Hancock and read to the assembled American army at New York.

Who gave the Library a copy of the Bill of Rights?

Barney Balaban purchased a copy of the Bill of Rights from rare book dealer Dr. A. S. W. Rosenbach. Balaban presented the document to the Library in February 1945 in "humble gratitude toward the freedom found by my parents when they came to this country seventy years ago." It is one of the copies Congress submitted to each of the colonies and is signed by the principal officers of the House and the Senate. John Beckley's signature as Clerk of the House is significant since he was appointed Librarian three years later.

Who sold the Library a copy of "The Star Spangled Banner"?

On October 15, 1940, the Library acquired a copy of the first published version of "The Star Spangled Banner." It was discovered in an old scrapbook in the attic of Jesse L. Cassard of Baltimore who sold it to the Library. On September 13, 1814, attorney Francis Scott Key boarded a British warship in Baltimore harbor to negotiate the exchange of prisoners but was detained until the end of the bombardment. During the bombardment, he sketched a preliminary version of the song on an envelope and the poem was printed a few days later in a Baltimore newspaper. The Library also has an 1840 manuscript copy of the poem in Keys's handwriting.

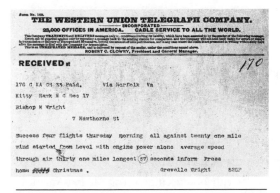

Bishop M. Wright received these heavenly tidings from son Orville to "inform press" after the first successful flight in 1903.

What telegram reporting mechanical failure changed the twentieth century?

The Library owns a telegram from a mechanic sent on December 15, 1903. It announces that a test conducted that day had resulted in a broken rudder but would be successful next time. Orville Wright sent it to his father in Dayton, Ohio, and made the first successful air flight two days later.

What manuscript copy of a famous novel by Somerset Maugham did the author give to the Library?

W. Somerset Maugham gave the Library *Of Human Bondage* to express his gratitude for America's hospitality in providing for English women and children evacuated during World War II.

What condition did Maugham make when he presented the Library with his manuscript of The Artistic Temperament of Stephen Carey?

Maugham also gave his manuscript copy of *The Artistic Temperament of Stephen Carey* to the Library in 1951. It bears the inscription: "This manuscript is presented to the Library of Congress on the condition that it is never to be printed." Maugham observed that if the Library had not accepted the manuscript, he would have destroyed it. Maugham reworked the theme of his manuscript and turned it into *Of Human Bondage.*

What did Fanny McConnell Ellison donate to the Library?

The widow of Ralph Ellison, author of *Invisible Man,* gave the Library 140 cartons of her husband's papers, both published and unpublished, in addition to his working library. The Library's Ralph Ellison Room contains his books.

How extensive is the Booker T. Washington Collection?

Over 180,000 items.

When did the Library acquire it?

In 1943 from Tuskegee Institute. The gift of this prime source of African-American history made these documents accessible to all Americans.

What other African-American collection does the Library own?

Records of the NAACP. Manuscripts from the National Urban League. And collections from the Harmon Foundation of New York (with its concentration on African-American artists and African art). The Library also owns the papers of Arthur Spingarn, founder of the NAACP.

What is the Library's largest manuscript collection?

Records of the NAACP. They fill 5,375 boxes and are still growing. It is also the most heavily used collection in the Manuscript Reading Room.

How did the Library get the papers of Thurgood Marshall?

After his resignation as Supreme Court Justice, Thurgood Marshall began to burn some of his papers. Then, he recalled a letter from the Library of Congress twenty-seven years earlier suggesting that he donate his papers. Justice Marshall told his secretary to call the Library.

Expert Witness: In 1934, Post Office officials brought a phostostat copy of Sir Francis Drake's will to the Library with the request that its Latin text be translated. A member of the Library's Manuscript Division went to Sioux City as an expert witness and testified at the trial of a man accused of swindling people out of hundreds of thousands of dollars. The defendant had convinced them that they were legal heirs to the estate of Sir Francis's son. The guilty party was sentenced to ten years' imprisonment. In truth, Sir Francis never had a son.

Whose walking stick was left to the Library?

In 1947, Dr. Samuel Johnson's walking stick was presented to the Library by Florence Bayard Hilles of Wilmington. It is thirty-seven and one-half inches long and made from the polished black horn of an oryx. A silver snuff box forms the head with crystalline quartz from Scotland set in its lid, which bears the inscription "Dr. Samuel Johnson 1760." Attached to the walking stick is a long cord with a dark tassel. In his famous *Dictionary of the English Language,* Dr. Johnson lists a "walking staff." Dr. Johnson put this instrument to good use when he was beset by four muggers on a dark London street. The authorities came to his rescue "and carried both him and them" into custody.

What chilling document from the French Revolution does the Library own?

A list of the citizens executed by guillotine master Samson. Attached to each name is the fee for his services.

What are some other notable manuscript collections at the Library?

The list includes:

Alexander Graham Bell

Edward Bernays

Black Abolitionist Papers

Louis D. Brandeis

William J. Brennan

Edward W. Brooke

Luther Burbank

Vannevar Bush

James M. Cain

Andrew Carnegie

Octave Chanute

Stuart Chase

James H. Doolittle

W. E. B. Du Bois

Ira Eaker

Edward Everett

German Captured Materials
    (Himmler Papers)

Grosvenor Family

William F. Halsey

Alexander Hamilton

Averell Harriman

Harold Ickes

Henry Kissinger
    (97 percent restricted)

Charles A. Lindbergh

Raymond Loewy

Groucho Marx

Margaret Meade

James A. Michener

Henry Morgenthau, Sr.

Daniel P. Moynihan

Edward R. Murrow

Frederick Law Olmsted

J. Robert Oppenheimer

George S. Patton

John J. Pershing

Pinkerton National
    Detective Agency

Vincent Price

Puerto Rican Memorials

Ayn Rand

Asa Philip Randolph

Donald Regan

Eddie Rickenbacker

Russian Church in Alaska

Bayard Rustin

Eric Sevareid

Shaker Collection

Carl Spaatz

Henry L. Stimson

Daniel Webster

Mae West

Wilbur and Orville Wright

Here is a first draft of Charles Lindbergh's *The Spirit of St. Louis.* The Library also has documents from another famous Atlantic crosser, Christopher Columbus.

Librarian Mumford shows the creators of "Some Enchanted Evening" (Richard Rodgers and Oscar Hammerstein) that once the Library owns your papers, it never lets them go.

What Stradivari instruments does the Music Division own?

It owns the Gertrude Clarke Whittall Collection that includes three violins, a cello, and a viola donated by Mrs. Whittall between 1935 and 1937. One of the violins was said to have belonged to Richard Wagner. The instruments are housed in a large glass display case in the Whittall Pavilion adjoining the Coolidge Auditorium.

What flute collection does the Music Division own?

It owns the Dayton C. Miller Flute Collection that includes 1,600 flutes, 10,000 pieces of music, 3,000 books, and 70 small sculptures of flutists. The flutes are from all countries and civilizations ranging from ancient Egypt to contemporary America. They are made from all types of material, including human bones, and include such curiosities as walking sticks that can be played. The showpiece is a mid-eighteenth century ebony and ivory flute (with porcelain case) that composer-king Frederick the Great of Prussia played.

Who was Dayton C. Miller?

He was a professor of physics specializing in acoustics who taught at the Case Institute of Physics in Cleveland, Ohio.

What is the history of the Kreisler violin?

Fritz Kreisler presented his Guarneri violin and Hill bow to the Library on April 14, 1952. The violin has a history of its own. Made about 1730 by Giuseppe Guarneri del Gesu, a contemporary of Stradivari, it supposedly came into the possession of Marshal Junot, one of Napoleon's commanders, who sent it by ship from Bordeaux to Lisbon. The ship was captured by a British privateer, and the violin taken by a sailor who sold it to a parson in Cumberland. It then passed through other hands until its acquisition by Kreisler.

Violinist Fritz Kreisler putting on a brave smile as he plays his priceless Guarneri for Librarian Evans before donating it to the Library in 1952.

How many books and manuscripts does the Music Division own?

The Music Division's holdings number over 6 million items in all spoken languages but none from Asia. The collections are comprehensive in American and European music. Composers who have deposited their archives include Irving Berlin (over 750,000 items), Leonard Bernstein, Aaron Copland, George and Ira Gershwin, Richard Rodgers, and John Philip Sousa. There are also original manuscripts by Bach, Haydn, Mozart, Beethoven, Schubert, Liszt, Brahms, and others.

What volume popularly known as the "Gutenberg Bible of Music" does the Library own?

Printed in 1504 in Venice, *Harmonice musices odhecaton A* is one of the first printed books with musical notes, published by Ottaviano dei Petrucci. Its title translated is: "One hundred songs in harmonic music." The letter A indicates that this is the first of a projected series.

When did the Music Division begin collecting opera librettos?

In 1908, the Music Division purchased more than 12,000 German and Italian librettos from a collector in Germany. Many more have been added since. In 1914, the Library published a catalog listing more than 6,000 librettos published before 1800 alone.

What forger fooled the Music Division?

In 1934, Tobia Nicotra sold a Mozart manuscript to the Music Division at a bargain price. It turned out to be too good to be true. Researchers discovered that Nicotra had ripped out blank pages from an old book of manuscripts and imitated the hand of fourteen-year-old Wolfgang Amadeus in faded ink. Other Nicotra fakes had already been uncovered by Walter Toscanini, son of the conductor and himself a Milan bookdealer. Nicotra was sentenced to two years in prison by an Italian court.

How was Beethoven's manuscript for his Piano Sonata (Opus 109) preserved?

The manuscript had a large inkblot made by the composer who was not famous for neatness. Preservation specialists removed the stain because its acidic content would have caused the manuscript to deteriorate.

What did music librarians discover about Beethoven's math?

The Music Division has a facsimile of a conversation book kept by the deaf composer. His notes reveal that his difficulty with math went much to the profit of his servant. To pay his servant's wages, Beethoven needed to multiply 36 by 4. He could only do this by adding 36 four times. The figure he obtained was 224.

Sheet music from the Heskes Collection for a Yiddish song commemorating the Titanic. On the cover, the owner of Macy's Department Store and his wife who died together are seen crowned by an angel.

What did music librarians discover about Paganini's concert fees?

Nicolò Paganini's fifteen London concerts earned him over 10,000 pounds. Statements found in notebooks kept in the Music Division show that he deposited over 14,000 pounds in London banks between 1832 and 1834. This was an enormous sum in those days.

How did the Library come to the aid of Arturo Toscanini?

Conductor Arturo Toscanini stopped the music when he rehearsed Carl Maria von Weber's *Invitation to the Dance* with the New York Philharmonic in July 1933. The maestro insisted that the musicians were playing a false note. The musicians resumed and again, Toscanini stopped them. The bewildered musicians appealed to the maestro and showed him the score. Toscanini refused to be pacified and told his secretary to call Dr. Carl Engel, head of the Library's Music Division. The secretary sang the thirteenth measure of Felix Weingarten's orchestration of the Weber piece over the telephone. Engel located the original copy of Weber's composition. Toscanini was proven right. Weingarten had substituted an eighth note followed by a quarter note for the short grace note followed by a doffed quarter note that Weber wrote down.

From the Heskes Collection, this song album (1910) influenced Yiddish stage star Fannie Brice, who was played by Barbra Streisand in the movie *Funny Girl* (1968).

Of what classical composer does the Music Division have the largest collection?

Johannes Brahms. Only the Gesellschaft der Musikfreunde of Vienna has a collection of comparable size.

Of what modern composer does the Music Division have the largest collection?

Leonard Bernstein. His collection contains almost 500,000 items. His papers were arranged by his piano teacher who later became his secretary.

What composers' furniture does the Music Division own?

George Gershwin's piano and customized desk with built-in pencil sharpener. It also owns a beautifully inlaid desk with glass top and a chair covered with brocade that belonged to Rachmaninoff.

What else does the Library own from Rachmaninoff?

In 1950, the widow of Sergei Rachmaninoff (1873–1943) gave the Library a large collection of his manuscripts, letters, and other memorabilia. Included in the manuscripts were the *Fourth Piano Concerto, Corelli Variations, Paganini Rhapsody, Third Symphony,* and *Symphonic Dances.*

What was the first recording acquired by the Library?

A 1904 wax cylinder recording the voice of Kaiser Wilhelm II of Germany.

What notable recordings does the Library own?

Recordings from the Berliner Gramaphone Company that invented disc recording.

Two hundred rare operatic recordings from pre-Revolutionary Russia (the Joel Berger Collection).

100,000 Office of War Information (OWI) discs made during World War II.

U.S. Marine Corps Combat Records made on Pacific islands during 1943–45 with eyewitness accounts of battles, including Iwo Jima.

Over 175,000 discs made between 1933 and 1979, including 80,000 broadcasts, World War II programs, presidential speeches, and the Olympic Games (the NBC Radio Collection).

What are recent additions to the Recorded Sound Section?

The Altschuler Jazz Collection with 220,000 78-rpm discs recorded from 1917 to 1950, one of the most comprehensive holdings of American jazz, blues, and popular music.

The Ella Fitzgerald Collection with over 10,000 music scores.

What unfinished business did Jelly Roll Morton leave at the Library?

Jelly Roll Morton was playing at a small club in Washington and participated in the Library's first oral history project. He cooperated by coming day after day to record his story and then disappeared. The last five years of his life are thus lost.

This bronze of Ella Fitzgerald has just been uncrated after being donated to the Library. Ella was the First Lady of "scat," the vocal equivalent of improvised jazz solos. Ed Dwight is the sculptor, the donor Geraldine Freund.

Why does the Music Division have a larger collection of Cuban dance band music than found in Cuba?

Fidel Castro destroyed Cuban dance band music recordings and prohibited their performance because they were considered decadent.

Can you listen to recordings in the Music Division?

Listening booths are reserved for those working on research projects. Casual music lovers are not served.

Are there musical performances at the Library?

The Library has given chamber music recitals since 1924. They were first sponsored and paid for by Elizabeth Sprague Coolidge who also gave the Library $60,000 to build an auditorium. The Budapest String Quartet was the first musical group to give scheduled recitals there. Since 1962, the Juilliard String Quartet has regularly performed.

"Mood Indigo," the piece Duke Ellington wrote and introduced in 1930 as "Dreamy Blues," is housed in the Library's massive collection of sheet music.

What is notable about the Coolidge Auditorium?

Completed in 1925, the Coolidge Auditorium in the Jefferson Building has perfect acoustics. Few recital halls in the United States are its equal.

What historical event was reenacted in the Coolidge Auditorium?

On May 2, 1950, a scene from Tom Taylor's *Our American Cousin* was performed. Before the curtain rose, Dr. Otto Eisenschiml, noted biographer, narrated step-by-step plans to murder President Lincoln. When the curtain rose, the cast wore original costumes from that fatal evening at Ford's Theater. No detail was lacking. Mr. Lincoln, wrapped in a shawl, sat in his rocking chair beside his wife and guests in the presidential box. After the shot fired by Dr. Eisenschiml in his dual role as narrator-assassin, the audience heard the clatter

of get-away hooves in the alley. It was noted that actor Edward Mangum, as Lincoln, "was so striking a likeness that he might well have confused Mathew Brady himself."

What has the American Folklife Center done to preserve American folk music?

Since 1928, the Center has sent out field workers to record, collect, and preserve American folk songs, ballads, and ethnic traditions.

Music stars from the Gershwin Collection: (clockwise) Blossom Seeley, George Gershwin, Paul Whiteman, Deems Taylor, and Ferde Grofé.

Music Writer: The Music Division has scores copied in Jean-Jacques Rousseau's hand. From 1750 to 1778, Rousseau earned his living copying music at 50 centimes (about 10 cents) a page. He kept a record of his copying, which shows that he copied over 11,000 pages!

THE MOTION PICTURE DIVISION

What is the first copyrighted film?

Fred Ott's Sneeze, shot in Edison's laboratory in 1893. Fred Ott was a lab employee noted for his antics.

How many films of Theodore Roosevelt does the Motion Picture, Broadcasting and Recorded Sound Division have?

The National Park Service donated 375 films documenting Theodore Roosevelt's life from 1909 to 1919.

In what Hollywood comedy does the Library of Congress appear?

In the 1950 film *Born Yesterday* with Judy Holliday and William Holden. Closeups show Miss Holliday standing by the Neptune Fountain, going through Library exhibits, and standing before the shrine containing the Declaration of Independence and the Constitution.

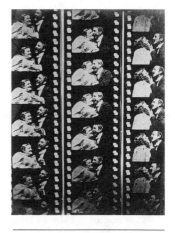

Featured in the American Memory Exhibition, these frames from Thomas Edison's film *The Kiss* (1896) show the first screen smooch in motion picture history.

Gregory Peck was spellbound by film preservation quality at the Library of Congress.

In what Hollywood thriller does the Library of Congress appear?

In the 1952 film *The Thief* starring Ray Milland. Milland is observed seemingly search-ing through a card catalog in the Main Reading Room until he can pass a roll of micro-film to a spy. The film is chiefly remembered for containing no dialogue.

What other Hollywood films use Library locations?

The West Point Story and *All the President's Men*, in which *Washington Post* reporters look through book slips containing requests by readers.

What scene in All the President's Men *was inaccurate?*

The scene shows *Washington Post* reporters Woodward and Bernstein played by Robert Redford and Dustin Hoffman asking to see loan records showing what books had been borrowed by the White House. Library loan records are confidential and no such event ever took place.

What silent screen star gave her entire film collection to the Library?

Mary Pickford donated all her personal films. The Mary Pickford Theater in the Jefferson Building has public screenings on a regular basis.

What famous singer is named on an application to appear with "the 3 Flashes" on "Major Bowes' Amateur Hour," a popular radio show of the 1930's and 1940's?

The application names Frank Sinatra as lead vocalist. The quartet, originally called "Frank Sinatra and the 3 Flashes," won the competition on September 8,1935. They toured a while for Major Bowes who changed their name to the "Hoboken Four." But Frank soon left to strike out on his own.

What are the terms of the National Film Preservation Act?

Under this act, the Librarian of Congress names twenty-five "culturally, historically, or aesthetically" significant motion pictures to the National Film Registry each year.

Bill "Hopalong Cassidy" Boyd visits good guy L. Quincy "Librarian of Congress" Mumford in 1955 to hand over two Western films.

What is the National Film Registry?

The definitive list of American motion pictures thought to be the finest examples of cinema's first century. They include Hollywood features; documentaries; avant-garde and amateur productions; films of regional interest; and ethnic, animated, and short film subjects.

What happens to any film named to the National Film Registry?

It is permanently restored at the Library's film preservation program in Dayton, Ohio, or through joint efforts with other film libraries, studios, and independent producers.

Why is this program necessary?

Fifty percent of all films made before 1950 and 90 percent of all films made before 1920 have been lost through fading and nitrate deterioration.

What are some historic voices you can hear at the Library?

The list includes:

P. T. Barnum	Rudyard Kipling
Sarah Bernhardt	Harry Lauder
Edwin Booth	David Lloyd George
William Jennings Bryan	Robert Edwin Peary
Buffalo Bill	John J. Pershing
Calvin Coolidge	Tyrone Power, Sr.
Thomas A. Edison	Victorien Sardou
Samuel Gompers	Sir Ernest Henry Shackleton
Warren G. Harding	William Howard Taft
Will H. Hays	Ellen Terry
O. Henry	Leo Tolstoy
Robert Green Ingersoll	Sir Herbert Beerbohn Tree
Henry Irving	Booker T. Washington
Joseph Jefferson	Stephen Samuel Wise

Bob Hope, who later donated his 100,000-joke file to the Library, is seen here dishing out a sample to Vice President Henry A. Wallace at the Hollywood Canteen during World War II.

THE PRINTS AND PHOTOGRAPHS DIVISION

How many items are in the Prints and Photographs Division?

Fifteen million items. This includes glass-plate negatives, stereographs, fine prints dating from the fifteenth century, architectural plans, and posters.

What are some of the more famous photographs?

There is a daguerreotype of thirty-seven-year-old Abraham Lincoln in Springfield, Illinois; thousands of Mathew Brady shots of the Civil War; 30,000 stereographs of nineteenth-century life; 300 glass-plate negatives recording Wright brothers' experiments; photos of life during the Great Depression; pictorial records from World Wars I and II, including captured German collections; 300,000 photos from the Office of War Information; and forgotten shots from American newspaper and magazine morgues.

In the print collection are thousands of political, commercial, and art posters; etchings and fine prints by Dürer, Rembrandt, Whistler, and others; architectural plans for the U.S. Capitol; records of the Historic American Buildings Survey;

and architectural drawings by such American masters as Frank Lloyd Wright and designer Raymond Loewy.

How did the Prints and Photographs Division acquire the Mathew Brady glass-plate negatives?

In 1944, the Library bought 7,500 glass-plate negatives taken by Brady and his assistants. Of these, 3,750 are photographs of the Civil War. About 2,650 represent portraits taken in the field or in the studio. Brady had turned over the pictures to a firm to which he was indebted. The firm in turn sold the collection to Alexander Gardner, a former Brady employee who added 2,000 more negatives. These were sold and ended up in Springfield, Massachusetts, stored next to a coal bin until 1942 when the storage building's owners, the Phelps Publishing Company, heard of the Library's eagerness to purchase the Brady collection.

What photographer got exclusive rights to sell his prints of murals and views of the new Library Building?

Levin C. Handy, nephew and apprentice of Civil War photographer Mathew Brady, was permitted to sell his photographs from a large ornate table in the Library. For more than thirty years, he was a familiar figure in the Jefferson Building. When the Library needed photographic copies of its material, Handy was the obvious photographer. He provided similar service for the War Department and the Department of State. Handy was the forerunner of the Library's Photo Duplication Service. He died in 1932.

What famous photographer donated his work to the Library?

In 1995, the distinguished photographer Gordon Parks donated his entire work to the Library. Parks was one of the first photographers to document African-American life. One of his most memorable portraits entitled "American Gothic" is

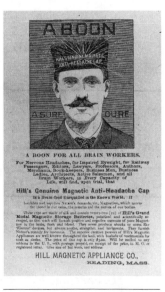

This magnetic cap cured aches and pains, not to mention what it did to dental fillings. Another health remedy from the Patent Medicine Label collection of the Prints and Photographs Reading Room.

of Ella Watson, a cleaning woman in the nation's capital standing in front of a large American flag, a mop in her left hand, a broom in her right. Parks who worked many years for *Life* has fifteen books in print and seven motion pictures and five documentaries to his credit.

How was the Prints and Photographs Division's panorama of the San Francisco earthquake taken?

George Lawrence suspended his camera from a fifty-pound kite to take this 1906 shot. The motto for his studio was "The Hitherto Impossible in Photography is Our Specialty."

What can Van Gogh scholars find at the Library?

The Library has two sketchbooks by nineteenth-century artist Ando Hiroshige whose works influenced Vincent Van Gogh. The sketchbooks were donated by Crosby Stuart Noyes in 1905. He was editor and publisher of the *Washington Star.* Altogether, Mr. Noyes donated several hundred Japanese prints, drawings, and 658 illustrated books.

How many photographs of Hermann Goering does the Library own?

The American military confiscated over 18,000 photographs of the Number Two Nazi after World War II and gave them to the Library.

How many Look magazine photographs does the Library own?

Among its many files from defunct magazines, the Library owns 5 million photographs from *Look.*

GEOGRAPHY AND MAP

Who conceived of the idea of a Geography and Map Division at the Library?

Lieutenant Edward B. Hunt of the U.S. Army formulated a detailed plan at the annual meeting of the American Association for the Advancement of Science held at Cleveland, Ohio, on July 28–August 2, 1853. He proposed that a special geographical library containing materials relating to America and the world at large would be of great value to history, commerce, and foreign relations. The Library of Congress was then proposed as the place where the plan could best be executed.

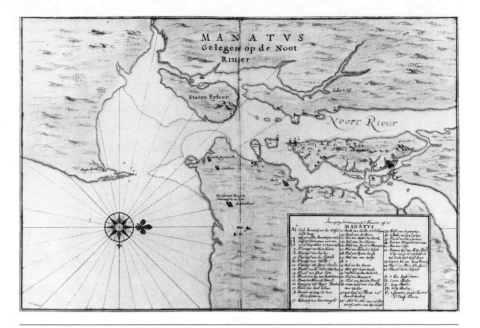

In the Geography and Map Division is the earliest known map of Manhattan. Place names are in Dutch and the island is referred to as Manatus.

How many maps does the Geography and Map Division own?

Over 4.5 million maps, some 60,000 atlases, and more than 350 globes. On average, 50,000 maps are added each year. Storing maps of such size and quantity requires a two-acre facility two floors below street level in the Madison Building.

What is one of the most valuable globes in the Division's collection?

In front of the Mumford Room of the Madison Building are two globes made by Venetian priest Vincenzo Maria Coronelli (1650-1718). One is celestial, the other terrestrial. The celestial globe shows the constellations and signs of the zodiac in bold colors. The terrestrial globe is surprisingly accurate, showing the Great Lakes and the Mississippi. Both are reductions of a pair of fifteen-foot globes Coronelli had made for Louis XIV of France. The originals were large enough to enclose a man.

What are some of the Division's most outstanding maps?

Maps of the American Revolution; a map of Caribbean currents compiled by Benjamin Franklin; hand-drawn Civil War maps used by generals of the Union and Confederate forces; and 700,000 fire insurance maps produced by the Sanborn Map Company. These large-scale fire insurance maps detail 12,000 American towns and cities.

What are some of the Division's more unusual items?

A book with a built-in compass and nine nautical maps made by Battista Agnese of Genoa, including one showing Magellan's route around the world. Also, some small, World War II silk maps with texts in foreign languages. These maps were issued to help American servicemen identify themselves to friendly civilians.

What presidential maps does the Library own?

George Washington made almost 150 maps as a surveyor. The Library owns about forty of them.

What founding father discovered the Gulf Stream?

In 1935, Franklin Bache, a direct descendant of Benjamin Franklin, presented the Library with a map made by Dr. Franklin in 1785 that showed the Gulf Stream flow. It was widely acknowledged that Franklin was one of the first to suspect the Gulf Stream's existence and to verify it by scientific observation. Franklin wrote: "Vessels are sometimes retarded, and sometimes forwarded in their voyages by currents at sea, which are often not perceived." Mariners had long been puzzled why a ship sailing from England to New York took two weeks longer than a ship sailing from New York to England.

What other uses did colonials find for powder horns?

The Geography and Map Division has eight powder horns dating from the colonial period and years of the American Revolution. They are inscribed with maps, names of towns, and sites of military campaigns. One horn, probably owned by a member of the militia, shows the Hudson and Mohawk River Valleys and bears a British coat of arms.

What mapmaker led "Stonewall" Jackson to victory?

General "Stonewall" Jackson acknowledged the invaluable maps produced by Major Jedediah Hotchkiss (1828–1899), a topographical engineer with the Confederate States Army. The Library acquired these maps in 1948. The most outstanding item is a field sketch book containing more than one hundred pages of maps, most of them drawn while the major was on horseback. Many of the Hotchkiss manuscripts are so finely drawn they give the appearance of printed maps.

What rare Eskimo map does the Library own?

A map prepared in 1925 by Silas Sandgreen, an Eskimo hunter. This aboriginal map-maker had never seen other maps and received no instructions from non-natives for his map of the Islands in Disko Bay on the west coast of Greenland. Constructed of sealskin, it includes individual islands whittled from Siberian driftwood. Sandgreen used yellow to represent grass and swamps; blue for lakes; and black for ground covered with black lichens.

What role have Library maps played in international disputes?

Library of Congress maps have resolved international disputes. In London, they settled the Alaska boundary questions. In 1925–1926, the Netherlands and the United States used Library maps to settle a dispute concerning the Island of Palmas in the Philippines.

What is unusual about some of the Division's Chinese maps?

Several maps donated by Andrew W. Mellon of Pittsburgh in 1930 are unusually large. One is eighty feet long. Another is sixty feet long and shows a one-hundred mile mountain highway.

What map more than any other is the Library of Congress's Most-Wanted?

A map made by Martin Waldseemüller that is the first to show America. The only known copy of this map is in Castle Wolfsegg, Germany.

A Whimsical Representation of England and Wales

What Library maps are in the shape of humans or animals?

There is a map of Britain in the shape of a woman on the back of a fish. A map of Europe is in the shape of Queen Elizabeth I. Switzerland is represented in the form of a bear and Belgium as a lion.

This rare find from the Geography and Map Division shows an old woman in the shape of Britain riding a fish and clutching a trident symbolizing England's mastery of the seas.

RARE BOOKS

What is on the bronze doors of the Rare Book and Special Collections Reading Room?

Six panels illustrating printer's marks from the time of Gutenberg to the twentieth century. The two bronze doors leading to the Rare Book and Special Collections Reading Room bear the marks of eminent printers. The top panel on the left shows the device of Johann Fust and Peter Schoeffer of Mainz, Germany, who took over from Gutenberg. Below it is the emblem of Geoffroy Tory, sixteenth-century French type and book designer. At the bottom is the mark of England's William Morris who founded the Kelmscott Press in 1891.

The top panel of the door on the right bears the names of founder Juan Cromberger and printer Juan Pablos who in 1539 operated the first press in the Americas in Mexico City. The center panel bears the names of Stephen Daye who became New England's first printer in 1640; William Nuthead, founder of Virginia and Maryland presses; and William Bradford, founder of the first press in New York and Pennsylvania. The bottom panel honors Bruce Rogers, twentieth-century American type and book designer.

What is the oldest written artifact in the Library?

A Sumerian cuneiform tablet dating from 2040 B.C.

What is the oldest African text in the Library?

Egyptian papyri with hieroglyphics written about 2000 B.C.

What is the oldest Biblical text in the Library?

A fragment of the *Book of Isaiah* from about the fourth century A.D. The text is in Greek and believed to have been written in Egypt.

What is the oldest printed book in the Library?

Not the Gutenberg Bible but a Chinese work entitled *Pai K'ung liu t'ieh*, which was printed around 1190, some 260 years before Gutenberg. Chinese printers, however, did not use a printing press but instead rubbed paper placed over engraved woodblocks brushed with ink.

What Columbus letter does the Library own?

Columbus wrote a letter to the Spanish court relating discoveries on his first voyage. The letter was translated into Latin, published, and disseminated throughout Europe. Although the original letter has been lost, the Library owns a 1493 copy printed in Rome.

What other Columbus rarity does the Library own?

Prior to his fourth and fifth voyages, Columbus called several judges and notaries to his Seville home to authenticate copies of documents by which the king and queen of Spain granted titles, revenues, and privileges to him and his heirs. These thirty-six original documents are known as *Columbus's Book of Privileges*. Written on vellum, they were bought from the son of Edward Everett who found them in Florence, Italy.

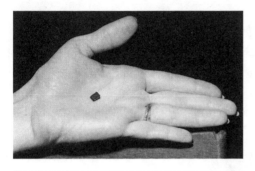

Pocket editions can't compete with this version of *The Rose Garden of Omar Khayyam* from the Library's collection of miniature books.

What is the smallest book in the Library?

An edition of *Old King Cole*. It is 1/25" x 1/25" or about the size of the period at the end of this sentence. The pages can be turned only by using a needle.

What is the largest book in the Library?

The first edition of John James Audubon's *Birds of America*. The book is over three feet high.

What is the oldest example of printing in the Library?

Three Japanese prayer charms known as dharani printed from copper blocks before A.D. 770. They are survivors of a million very small dharani published by order of the empress Shotoku. These prayer charms were placed in wooden containers carved to resemble miniature temples.

Printing in Asia was done by metal type or carved letters on woodblocks.

Gutenberg had no knowledge of the technology used in China, Korea, and Japan when he invented his printing press with metal letters cast from a mold.

What is the architectural style of the Rare Book Reading Room?

It is modeled after a colonial Georgian room in Philadelphia's Independence Hall. The three arches separating the Reading Room from the foyer are fashioned after the arches leading into the Pennsylvania Supreme Court Room in Independence Hall. The Doric columns are like those in Independence Hall's Assembly Room where the Declaration of Independence was signed. The Windsor armchairs for readers are similar to chairs in Independence Hall.

What famous artist designed a Library bookplate?

Rockwell Kent's futuristic rendering was submitted with the artist's statement: "If the name of the Library should ever be changed—and it certainly should be, to my mind, the Public Library of the United States of America—it would only be necessary to change the border of my bookplate design."

Librarian Mumford (center) receives *The Bay Psalm Book* donated by Mrs. Annie Jean Van Sinderen shown here with her son.

What is the rarest American book in the Library?

The Bay Psalm Book, the first book printed in the American colonies. It was published in 1640 by Stephen Daye at Cambridge in the Massachusetts Bay Colony. Only eleven copies have survived. One was owned by Thomas Prince, who began collecting early books and manuscripts as a student at Harvard in 1700. *The Bay Psalm Book* was passed on to his church where it lay in the attic until the nineteenth century when it was sold at auction. Alfred White, builder of the New York City subway, purchased the tattered volume and left it to his daughter, Annie Jean Van Sinderen, who donated it to the Library in 1967.

What colonial American publications were most popular after the Bible?

Next to the Bible, almanacs have the longest continuous history in American publishing. Farmers and townspeople found them indispensable for weather forecasts, phases of the moon, tidal tables, advice on planting and harvesting, and diversions such as riddles and proverbs. The Library has sixteen almanacs printed by Benjamin Franklin.

Dots and Dashes: The Library has the first telegraph tape ever sent. Samuel F. B. Morse sent it from the Supreme Court in the U.S. Capitol to the Baltimore rail depot. The message read: "What hath God wrought?"

Why was Britain's Magna Carta once kept at the Library?

Considered the finest of three copies signed in 1215 by King John and the barons, the Lincoln Cathedral copy of the Magna Carta was exhibited at the New York World's Fair in 1939. As World War II approached, the British government decided to deposit it at the Library of Congress for safekeeping. It was exhibited with the Declaration of Independence and the Constitution and returned to the British ambassador on January 11, 1946.

What are the two Lincoln Bibles?

The widow of Robert Todd Lincoln gave the Library two Bibles. The first, printed in Philadelphia in 1847, was the family Bible in which the president recorded deaths and births and other family history. The second, the inauguration Bible, was published in Oxford in 1853. It contains an inscription on the flyleaf stating that it was given by the Clerk of the Supreme Court to the Lincoln family. A certificate from the clerk to that effect appears on the back flyleaf.

Knowing that you can't keep a good man down, Harry Houdini prepares for burial at sea. He later donated his collection of books on magic and the occult to the Library.

What famous magician left his books and papers to the Library?

In 1927, Harry Houdini left his unique collection totaling more than 5,000 books on magic and the occult to the Library. The magician was known to buy a dealer's entire stock if certain books appealed to him, select what he wanted, and give away the rest to friends.

How many incunabula does the Library own?

The Library owns 5,700 books printed before 1501, the largest collection in the United States.

What book in the Library is the only copy in existence?

The *Doctrina Christiana*, a book of prayers published in Manila in 1593. It was the first book printed in the Philippines. Each section of the Spanish text is followed by text in Tagalog, a language native to the Philippines. The entire text was carved on woodblocks. The text had to be carved in reverse, block by block, and then printed by inking the raised letters and rubbing the blocks over paper. It is believed that the blocks were made by Chinese craftsmen since, centuries earlier, xylography or woodblock printing had been perfected in China. Undoubtedly, these Chinese craftsmen prepared the woodblocks under the supervision of Dominican fathers who composed the text consisting of the Lord's Prayer and other prayers in Spanish and Tagalog. The book was found in a Paris book shop after World War II and acquired by Lessing J. Rosenwald who presented it to the Library in 1947.

Shortly before his assassination, Lincoln breathed through straws to assist artist Clark Mills in preparing the only known life mask of the sixteenth president. This bronze cast from the mask was donated to the Library in 1970.

What are the most famous Lincoln memorabilia in the Library?

On display in the "American Treasures of the Library" exhibit are the following items found in the president's pockets on the night of his assassination: a handkerchief with the name "A. Lincoln" in red thread; a penknife; a watch fob; a cufflink; a leather wallet containing newspaper clippings; and a $5 Confederate banknote. Two pairs of glasses with a leather case and a lens wiper are also in this collection. Nothing reveals

Lincoln as less unpretentious than the piece of string tied to one of his eyeglass frames to hold them together.

What other Lincoln memorabilia does the Library own?

Two life masks, one of Lincoln made in April 1860 and the other of Stephen A. Douglas, his opponent in their famous debate. Both masks are part of the Alfred Whital Stern Collection of Lincolniana. Also in the collection are a pearl necklace and two bracelets, which the president gave to his wife Mary. The president purchased the jewelry from Tiffany and Co. on April 28, 1862, paying $180 for the necklace and $350 for the bracelets.

What other famous item of Lincolniana did the Library lose only to regain?

President Lincoln's famous letter appointing Major General Hooker as commander-in-chief of the army of the Potomac was sold at public auction in 1924. The Library offered $1,000 but the manuscript went for $10,000 and was resold for $15,000 in 1941. Alfred Whital Stern of Chicago later donated the letter to the Library where it is on permanent display in the Rare Book Reading Room.

What Library Treasures are on postage stamps?

The Post Office issued a Gutenberg Bible stamp on September 30, 1952 with a ceremony at the Library. *The Doctrina Christiana* appears on a Philippine stamp.

What manuscript book went on display at the Library on April 4, 1952, exactly five-hundred years to the day the scribe began work on it?

The Giant Bible of Mainz.

What is the Giant Bible of Mainz?

This two-volume manuscript Bible, completed in 1453, was kept in the library of Mainz Cathedral. In 1631, during the Thirty Years' War, it was seized by King Gustavus Adolphus of Sweden who gave it to one of his officers, Duke Bernhard of Saxe-Weimar. Later, it passed into the hands of the Dukes of Gotha. In 1952, it was sold to New York rare book dealer H. P. Kraus who sold it to Lessing J. Rosenwald of Jenkintown, Pennsylvania, with the understanding that it would eventually be placed in the Library of Congress.

Who wrote it?

We do not know the scribe's name. After finishing his task, he wrote on the last page: Calamus Fidelis (Faithful Pen). He completed the entire text in one year at the rate of one leaf per day. His pencil lines, to prevent him spilling into the margins, are still visible. The beautiful border illuminations with flowering vines, butterflies, birds, and deer, along with hunters and their dogs, are the work of two illuminators.

Is there any relationship between the Gutenberg Bible and the Giant Bible of Mainz?

Both Bibles are exhibited at the Library in opposite display cases because they are superb examples of manuscript books and the first printed books. Both use similar gothic lettering, and were produced at the same time in Mainz, without Calamus Fidelis or Gutenberg having known each other.

What is the most amazing thing about the Gutenberg Bible?

It is the first book printed in Europe and still one of the most beautiful books ever printed.

Where did the art of printing begin?

It began as early as the eighth century A.D. in China, Korea, and Japan. However, printing in Asia was not done on a press, nor were the letters produced from adjustable molds. In any case, Gutenberg had no knowledge of their methods.

How did Gutenberg develop the printing press?

He first devised a mechanical device that could produce metal letters of uniform size. Typefaces had to be set with such precision that they aligned perfectly on a uniform printing surface.

What inspired his invention?

He got his idea for the printing press from the wine press and the press used to squeeze water from paper during manufacturing.

How many metal letters did Gutenberg make?

About 46,000, enough to keep six presses busy.

How did he develop the right ink?

He modified the oil-based ink used by painters and developed printing ink that adhered to metal letters without smudging.

How long did it take him to develop the printing press?

About ten years.

How long did it take him to print the Bible?

Four years.

How many Bibles did he print?

About 180 paper copies and 35 vellum copies.

What are vellum copies?

They are made from very fine animal skins. About 140 skins make one volume. Gutenberg's 35 vellum copies used the skins of almost 5,000 animals.

How much did a Gutenberg Bible cost?

A vellum copy was 24 gulden, and a paper copy was 17 gulden. In those days, the price for a house in Mainz, Germany, where Gutenberg worked was was about 80 to 100 gulden.

How much did Gutenberg earn from printing?

He went bankrupt and died blind and almost forgotten.

How many Gutenberg Bibles still exist?

Forty-eight vellum and paper copies; eleven are in the United States.

What is special about the Library's Gutenberg Bible?

Printed about 1454, it is one of only three perfect vellum copies still in existence. Perfect means that there are no tears or leaves missing. The other two vellum copies are in Paris and London.

Who previously owned the Library's Gutenberg Bible?

Benedictine monks were the only previous owners. They kept it from about 1458 until 1930. In 1768, it was tossed from the windows of a German monastery to save it from fire. During the Napoleonic wars, the monks carried it to safety in Switzerland. When Switzerland was invaded, they carried it to Austria.

How much did the Library's Gutenberg Bible cost?

The Benedictines sold it for $370,000 to Otto Vollbehr, a German book dealer. Vollbehr then sold it to the Library along with 3,000 rare books for a total of $1.5 million. This sale was one of the best investment Congress ever made, a feat that can never be duplicated.

What did Vollbehr do with his windfall?

He netted very little of the proceeds as he was heavily in debt to others.

What kind of censorship did the Library's rare book curator discover?

In 1935, the curator found two pages of a 1483 German Bible sealed with wax. Between them, a woodcut showed Bathsheba fully dressed with her feet in a shallow basin. Her admirer, King David, is waving to her from a balcony. The mere suggestion of bare feet was too much for certain clerics who sealed the pages.

Who donated the Library's most valuable collection of books?

Between 1943 and his death in 1979, Lessing J. Rosenwald gave the Library 2,600 rare books and 15,000 other volumes. The value of his donation is estimated at well over $1 billion. Rosenwald was the classic collector: he had intimate knowledge of the works he collected and wanted to share his enjoyment with others. Nothing better illustrates his attitude toward books than the anecdote about insects that damaged a print he had lent to a South American exhibit. While the curators were understandably agitated, Rosenwald was heard to remark: "Better to be seen and eaten than not be seen at all."

What are some of the rarest items in the Rosenwald Collection?

The 48-line Bible produced by Fust and Schoeffer (the first dated Bible and first book to carry a printer's device or trademark); five books printed in the fifteenth century by William Caxton, England's first printer; a *Divina commedia* printed in Florence in 1481 (the first illustrated edition of Dante and one of the earliest books with copperplate engravings); and a unique collection of books written and illustrated by poet-artist William Blake, including the only known copy of the *The Book of Ahania*.

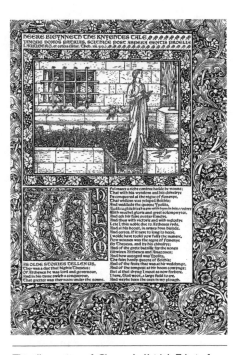

This illustration of Chaucer's *Knight's Tale* is from William Morris's famous edition of *The Canterbury Tales* in the Rare Book Room.

What is unusual about the room where the Rosenwald Collection is stored?

Located in the Jefferson Building, across from the Rare Book Room, the Rosenwald Room is a replica of Alverthorpe Gallery, the collector's library in Jenkintown, Pennsylvania. Even the fabric of the couch and pillows has been copied.

What important German collection captured in World War II is in the Rare Book Room?

Hitler's private library was confiscated by American troops and sent to the Library of Congress. Books with Hitler's pencil marks, as well as special editions and albums presented to the Führer, are included in this collection.

What is the Peter Force Collection?

With the 1867 purchase of Peter Force's library for $100,000, the Library obtained one of its great collections of Americana, as well as Colonial and Revolutionary documents. Included are 1,000 volumes of eighteenth- and nineteenth-century newspapers, over 22,000 books, 40,000 pamphlets, and more than 1,200 maps. Force bought many of the manuscripts as wastepaper after government offices disposed of them for scrap. Also included in his library were 429 volumes consisting of fifteenth- and sixteenth-century manuscripts, as well as incunabula, which began the Library's collection of fifteenth-century books.

Who was Peter Force?

Peter Force (1790–1868), publisher and historian, had been mayor of Washington, D.C., and a brigadier general in the District of Columbia militia.

What library started its Americana collection before the Library of Congress?

The British Museum realizing the value of Americana began collecting it when the Library of Congress still only concerned itself with legal material. By the mid-nineteenth century, the British Museum had purchased every published American book, pamphlet, sermon, school book, and children's story. With the purchase of the Peter Force Collection, the Library of Congress began its own Americana collection and soon surpassed the British Museum.

What is the Toner Collection?

In 1882, Joseph Toner, a physician of Washington, D.C., donated his library of 40,000 volumes to the Library of Congress. They were mostly medical works and local histories. It was the first great donation made to the Library and was accepted by a grateful Congress.

What did the Library purchase from Siberia?

In 1906, the Library acquired the library of liquor merchant, gold miner, and real estate tycoon Gennadius Vasilievich Yudin. This became the core of the Library's Slavic collection. In 1901, the Library owned 569 Russian books. In one stroke, the Yudin library brought the total to 80,000 volumes. It took over 500 specially constructed packing cases to ship these books to Washington.

How important did Russia consider the Yudin purchase?

Enough to clear railway lines from Siberia all the way across Russia to give Yudin's 80,000 books the right of way. The fact that Russian and Japanese delegates met at the Library in 1905 to settle the Russo-Japanese War resulted in Russia's good feelings toward the Library.

Who had used the Yudin Collection while exiled in Siberia?

V. I. Lenin.

What is of particular interest to Americans in the Yudin Collection?

It contains manuscripts on Russian exploration of the west coast of North America and Alaska.

What other collection came from Russia?

After the Russian Revolution, the czar's personal library was dispersed throughout Russia. A New York bookseller (with the Library of Congress in mind) bought 1,733 volumes from an agency authorized to sell them. Bound with the imperial bookplate, this collection included fifty volumes of documents compiled by the Russian General Staff.

How many miniature books does the Library own?

The Library's Rare Book and Special Collections Division owns 2,000 miniature books, i.e., books four inches or less in height.

Prize Catch: Among Presidential Library books is a "Hunting Library" that belonged to Theodore Roosevelt. This collection donated by the president's grandson, Kermit Roosevelt, includes rare classics from the sixteenth and seventeenth centuries. *The Historie of Serpents* printed by William Jaggard in London in 1608 shows an enormous boa swallowing a child. Fifteen years later, Jaggard printed the first Shakespeare Folio.

What did the widow of President Wilson give to the Library?

In 1946, Edith Bolling Wilson donated her husband's personal library of 9,000 volumes.

What is the most significant collection of Americana acquired in the twentieth century?

In 1996, the Library acquired by purchase and gift the Marian S. Carson Collection. It includes more than 10,000 manuscripts, broadsides, unpublished letters, and pre-Revolutionary documents. Also included are the first portrait photograph taken in the United States, a black-and-white chalk memorial portrait of George Washington made shortly after his death, an extremely rare broadside printing of the Declaration of Independence, and an 1856 watercolor of the Senate in session in the African republic of Liberia.

What discovery did a noted researcher make when he found strips tucked into the inner seam of a rare book?

Paul Needham, a scholar of rare books and early printing, saw that the strips made of vellum had printing on them. He requested the Library to have the book disbound so that he could examine the strips. They turned out to be parts of an indulgence issued by the Catholic Church for the remission of sins. It had been printed by William Caxton, England's first printer.

What happened to Walt Whitman's notebooks?

The Library sent Whitman's twenty-four notebooks and cardboard butterfly to a secret Ohio location for safekeeping during World War II. On their return in 1944, ten notebooks and the butterfly were missing. Four notebooks and the butterfly were recovered in January 1995 from a New York auction house.

What Whitman memorabilia does the Library own?

The country's largest collection of Whitman manuscripts (some 20,000), his walking stick, pocket watch, eyeglasses, and a leather pouch used for carrying gifts to wounded soldiers during the Civil War.

What is left of the original manuscript of Leaves of Grass?

Only page 10. On the back, Whitman left notes for a new poem published in the second edition. That may be the only reason page 10 survived.

What measures did the Library take to protect its collections during World War II?

Six months before Pearl Harbor, 700 Library staff worked 10,000 extra hours (an average of fourteen hours each). They selected irreplaceable works to be taken from the collections if an emergency occurred. When war broke out, the selected items were packed in 4,789 wooden cases. It took twenty-nine trucks to carry them to sites outside Washington.

What did the Sultan of Turkey give to the Library?

In 1884, Sultan Abdul-Hamid II gave the Library 375 books in specially bound volumes. These included photographs taken by a French firm depicting life at the Turkish palace and in the armed forces.

Not By Bread Alone: The Library's Near East Section has seventy manuscripts illustrating Arabic calligraphy. With these rarities is a small box containing a grain of rice and a grain of wheat. The kernels were sent from Saudi Arabia by an admirer of the Library. Each grain is hand-lettered with an inscription in Arabic. Only with strong magnification can the inscriptions be read.

On the rice kernel is written:

Denying rights leads to disobedience.
Favor is lost with the fool and the ignoble.

The wheat kernel bears the maxims:

Do not despise the weak of today for he may become great tomorrow. Tyranny and cruelty breed laziness and alienation.

Among the Library's smallest treasures are two inscriptions from the Koran on a rice kernel (top) and a grain of wheat. Both were donated by a Saudi admirer of the Library.

What unusual items are in the Library's Kipling collection?

Aside from first editions, manuscripts, and galley proofs with the author's corrections, the collection includes the autograph manuscript of *Mowgli's Brothers,* the first of the Jungle Stories. There are six "Kipling dinner plates." Each contains an original verse about the fruit Kipling painted on the china during a visit to America in 1899.

What book given to the Library in 1950 by Cecil B. DeMille cost $300,000 to research?

To provide historical accuracy for the film *Samson and Delilah*, Paramount engaged ten scholars over a fourteen-year period to research Philistine life from 1600 to 1200 B.C. Subjects ranged from abracadabra, bakers, caves, cosmetics, dinner parties, millstones, money, warfare, and the zodiac. The researchers consulted some thirty institutions, including the Library of Congress, and their reports are compiled in the book.

What rarities are in the Batchelder Collection?

The John Davis Batchelder Collection includes the first dictionary from the New World printed in Mexico City in 1555; autographs of Ferdinand and Isabella, Peter the Great, Jesse James, Jack Dempsey, John L. Sullivan, and Babe Ruth; first editions of Shakespeare and Charles Dickens; and books on magic and witchcraft.

Unusual Items at the Library of Congress:

An oarlock from the gondola used by Richard Wagner in Venice.

A lock of Beethoven's hair, which John Davis Batchelder had fixed with tape in his album.

A knife-fork-spoon-corkscrew combination used by Charles Dickens on his travels and his ivory-handled walking stick.

Coincidence: A reader asked for a book on Dutch theology published in 1602. It was the first time the book had ever been requested. The book could not be located until the staff discovered that another reader had borrowed it just a short time earlier.

What Library exhibit changed ideas about the origin of baseball?

Baseball is believed to have originated in 1839 in Cooperstown, New York. It may be time to revise the date. At the "John Bull & Uncle Sam" exhibit held at the Library in Winter 1999–2000, there was a very small children's book from the British Library entitled *A Pretty Little Pocket-Book Intended for the Amusement of Little Master Tommy, and Pretty Miss Polly* . . . (London, 1790). An earlier edition dates from 1744. On one of the pages is a woodcut of children playing with bat and ball. Beneath it is this poem:

B A S E - B A L L

The Ball once struck-off,

Away flies the Boy

To the next destin'd Post,

And then Home with Joy.

THE LAW LIBRARY

What are the origins of the Law Library?

The original 750 books in the Library of Congress were almost all devoted to law. They are the basis of the Library of Congress.

What distinguishes the Law Library from all other divisions?

Because of the number of readers, Library of Congress law books were moved to a separate "apartment" by order of President Andrew Jackson on July 4, 1832. The Law Library was under the jurisdiction of the Supreme Court until 1935.

Are all books in the Law Library devoted to American law?

No. Roughly half the collection is foreign law. The Law Library maintains the largest collection of legal material in the world. Part of the staff is composed of lawyers who are expert in foreign law. Thus, there are lawyers trained in the laws of European countries, the Middle East, Asia, Africa, and Latin America.

What is unique about the Law Library book stacks?

The book stacks are underground, covering a two-acre area. Some ninety-nine shelves are motor-driven to make maximum use of space. As much as eighty percent more space would have been needed if it were not for these movable shelves nine feet high on motorized tracks. If measured end to end, Law Library shelves would stretch for sixty miles.

What happened to Chief Justice Marshall in the Law Library's book stacks?

Chief Justice Marshall liked to get books from the shelves himself rather than ask for assistance. Once, a large volume struck him on the head and laid him out on the floor. Declining aid to get to his feet, the old gentleman said: "I've laid down the law out of the law books many a time in my long life, but this is the first time they have laid me down. I am completely floored."

Library Rules: In 1952, Colonel Webb of the Main Reading Room asked the Law Library for a ruling on personal property left behind by occupants of study rooms. The answer was provided by Law Librarian W. Lawrence Keitt and W. C. Rowe of the American-British Law Section in a twenty-four-page, single-spaced typescript.

Citing Old Testament law, Roman law, and federal and local precedents with extensive citations, the legal experts came to the conclusion that the owner should be notified and property held for thirty days. After sixty days, personal belongings would become "surplus government property."

What is the Oliver Wendell Holmes Devise Fund?

In his will (1935), Chief Justice Holmes left more than 14,000 volumes to the Law Library. The Fund publishes books devoted to Supreme Court history.

How does the Law Library assist Native Americans?

The Law Library maintains a comprehensive record of federal treaties with Native American tribes. An exceptional early twentieth-century source is the seven-volume *Indian Territory Reports, 1900–1909,* which include tribal constitutions and charters for more than 200 federally-recognized tribal groups.

THE HISPANIC DIVISION

What is the origin of the Hispanic Division?

After the war with Mexico in 1848, the Joint Committee on the Library authorized Librarian Meehan to purchase Mexican law books and newspapers. Congress needed information on the country where American troops were stationed.

What publication of the Hispanic Division is the most outstanding of its kind?

The *Handbook of Latin American Studies* contains contributions from over one hundred researchers who are experts in their fields. There are 6,000 annotations in each volume published annually. Volumes 1–53 are now available on CD-ROM.

What is unusual about Columbus's coat of arms in the Hispanic Reading Room?

It is said to be the first mural painted on steel and weighs approximately 1,200 pounds. It was a gift from the Allegheny Ludlum Steel Corporation. Originally, the king and queen of Spain chose Columbus's symbols, but he made an unauthorized alteration. His coat of arms depicts the royal arms of Castille and León consisting of a castle and lion. Another part was to have shown the origin of the Columbus family. Not wanting to reveal his ancestors' non-noble origins, Columbus filled the fourth part of his crest with five anchors.

What other murals are in the Hispanic Reading Room?

There are four murals depicting the civilizations of Spain and Portugal encountering the Americas. Brazilian artist Cândido Portinari was commissioned to paint them.

What are the motifs connecting these murals?

The motifs connecting them are the Work of the Spaniards and Portuguese in the New World: Discovery of the Land; Entry into the Forest; Teaching of the Indians; and Mining of Gold.

Who initiated the Library's service to the blind?

Librarian John Russell Young requested that accommodations be made for the blind and a room set aside for their use of braille books. In an August 18, 1897 memo to the superintendent of the Main Reading Room, Young wrote: "The idea is somewhat nebulous and there may be practical obstacles with which I am not familiar. At the same time, a special service for the blind would go far towards the idea of a national library."

When did the Library begin service to the blind?

The Library began to serve the blind as early as 1900, but it was not until 1931 that Congress passed specific legislation to serve blind readers. The program was expanded in 1952 to include children. In 1966, those with physical disabilities were included.

What does the Library provide for the blind and handicapped?

The National Library Service for the Blind and Physically Handicapped administers the circulation of braille books, as well as books on tape or "talking books." The Library also lends machines for cassettes. Over 22.6 million braille items circulate each year. These include discs, cassettes, and books.

What was the first braille book printed for the Library?

Woodrow Wilson's biography, *George Washington*.

Where did "talking books" get their start?

Books recorded on 33-1/3 rpm records got their start at the Library and were available to blind patrons in 1934, fourteen years before the concept of "talking books" was adopted by studios and sold commercially.

Thomas Alva Edison, inventor of the phonograph, listed "phonograph books" for the blind as the second of proposed uses for his 1877 patent application. Music was listed fourth.

When Edison first applied for a patent on his "phonograph or speaking machine," he described how such a device might "read" for the blind. It was not until 1934, however, that "talking books" were developed by the American Foundation for the Blind in New York City.

Who repairs the disc and cassette players sent to thousands of blind and handicapped patrons of the Library?

The Telephone Pioneers of America, a national association of senior and retired telephone workers, repair and maintain these machines on a volunteer basis.

How are cassettes, braille books, and magazines distributed?

The Library sends books and magazines in recorded form by postage-free mail. In addition, a network of designated libraries and regional libraries in each state distributes talking books. Some talking books are also available in Spanish, French, and other languages.

What does the Library provide for the Internal Revenue Service?

The Library produces braille copies of income tax forms complete with instructions and schedules.

COPYRIGHT

How did Copyright become part of the Library?

In 1815, a bill suggested by Librarian Watterston that authors and publishers deposit books and engravings at the Library rather than the Patent Office failed to pass a second Senate vote. However, in 1870, Librarian Spofford secured the Library's exclusive power to grant copyright. He little imagined that this addition to his duties would consume most of his time. He granted copyright to many famous American authors, including Walt Whitman and Mark Twain.

What label from a beverage advertised as a "valuable brain tonic and cure for all nervous affections—Sick Head Ache, Neuralgia, Hysteria, Melancholy" was copyrighted in 1887?

A label bearing the signature of John S. Pemberton, the Atlanta druggist who invented Coca-Cola in 1886, is on file in the Copyright Office. Coca-Cola's archivist in Atlanta confirmed that their copyright label is the earliest printed label used for the beverage.

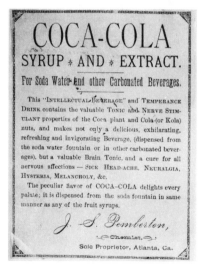

"Things go better with Copyright!" Here is the original Coca-Cola label signed on the back by the Atlanta druggist who concocted it.

What copyrighted song title by George M. Cohan had to be changed because of public outrage?

With its reference to the Stars and Stripes as a rag, the song "You're a Grand Old Rag" was retitled "You're a Grand Old Flag."

What gift did the Copyright Office give to Sir Winston Churchill?

Staff in the Library's Copyright Office were amazed to find that Winston Churchill had 556 claims. When he visited President Eisenhower at the White House on June 25, 1954, three Library representatives presented Sir Winston with a specially bound index to all his copyright claims. The index was entitled, *To the Rt. Hon. Sir Winston Churchill, K. G., in his Character as Voluminous Author.* Accepting the gift, he remarked that he still had a "modest" work to add to the index—a history of the English-speaking peoples in some 800,000 words.

What is the minimum age for obtaining copyright?

There is no minimum age. Children may obtain copyright.

How do you copyright a book?

You fill out a form, pay $30, and submit two copies of the published work or one copy if unpublished.

Can you copyright a mechanical device you have invented?

No. Work to be patented must be submitted to the Patent Office, which is under the jurisdiction of the Department of Commerce.

Can you copyright an idea?

No.

What else can you copyright besides books, plays, and music?

Photographs, engravings, prints, maps, clothing designs, sound recordings, choreography, computer programs, and hull designs for boats.

Where can you find an unequaled record of America's cultural and historical past in the Copyright Office?

The Copyright Office maintains a 41-million-card catalog open to the public. It is the largest file in the world. It contains individual cards recording all applications for copyright from 1870 to 1977. Also available on microfilm are 150,000 copyright registrations from 1790 to 1870. Records after 1979 are on microfiche and in electronic databases.

What rare picture of the Statue of Liberty was discovered in the Copyright Office?

In 1876, sculptor Frédéric Auguste Bartholdi registered his statue of "Liberty Enlightening the World." The statue is depicted as holding broken chains. In the sculptor's final version unveiled in 1886, the Statue of Liberty holds a tablet.

What did librarians find when they searched material for a Walt Disney exhibit held in 1990?

A Library warehouse contained more than one hundred rare model sheets showing Disney characters created between 1932 and 1945.

What famous movie prop is on display at the Library?

The Maltese Falcon. Warner Brothers used six copies of the famous bird for publicity shots of the 1941 film. One of the copies is exhibited outside the Library's Copyright Office in the Jefferson Building.

What movie star copyrighted a children's book when she was fourteen?

Elizabeth Taylor wrote and illustrated *Nibbles And Me* about her pet chipmunk.

To whom does the Copyright Office disburse several hundred million dollars each year?

By authority of the Digital Audio Home Recording Act, the Office collects license fees for cable television, satellite carriers, and digital audio recording devices. Royalties are collected, invested, and distributed to copyright holders of sound recordings and musical compositions and to certain performing artists.

CONGRESSIONAL RESEARCH SERVICE

The Congressional Research Service is modeled on plans from which state?

The Madison Building's reading room for congressional researchers is named after Wisconsin's Robert M. LaFollette who in 1914 introduced an amendment establishing a Legislative Reference Bureau at the Library.

What was the model for the Legislative Reference Bureau?

In 1901, Wisconsin created a legislative reference bureau modeled after the Kaiser's German prototype. As a presidential advisor noted to a House committee investigating similar research support for the federal government: "It is the German idea of having a scientific staff back of the line; and to my mind, it is the one thing that has made Germany more proficient than any other nation in its governmental processes."

What does the Congressional Research Service do?

Established in 1914 as the Legislative Reference Bureau, CRS is the oldest support agency of Congress. Its origins may be traced to 1806, when a book room in the Capitol was provided "to enable statesmen to be correct in their investigations." Today, CRS provides brief answers to inquiries from congressional offices and prepares detailed studies to analyze legislative issues. Topics range from social legislation to intricate questions on weapons systems. Staff in this division work under extreme deadlines. All research reports are unbiased and not permitted to reflect political party views. CRS provides facts but Congress makes decisions.

How many inquiries does the Congressional Research Service handle?

From 1915 to 1937, the Legislative Reference Service answered 33,283 inquiries. During 1999, CRS completed 545,663 research assignments for Congress.

How many people work for the Congressional Research Service?

A staff of 760 researchers responds to congressional requests.

THE NATIONAL DIGITAL LIBRARY

What is American Memory?

In June 1997, the Library awarded $600,000 to ten American libraries to digitize their collections of American historical materials for inclusion in American Memory.

What will the digitized collections of American Memory comprise?

From Library of Congress collections: African-American sheet music from 1870 to 1920; photographs of mining booms in Colorado; minstrels, spirituals, and musicals from Tin Pan Alley; agricultural settlements in the northern Great Plains; ex-slave narratives; and images from the Texas–Mexico border. American Memory is a public-private partnership funded by Congress and donations from a number of sponsors (including a $2-million gift from the Ameritech Foundation).

How can you see thousands of Library collections without leaving your home?

Hundreds of thousands of digitized items can be accessed on the Library's World Wide Web home page:

http://www.loc.gov.

Does the Library have a Web site for the classroom?

A Web site developed for educators from kindergarten through high school may be accessed on:

http://lcweb2. loc.gov/ammem/ndlpedu.

How many different databases are available to Library patrons?

Over ninety databases are online in the Computer Catalog Center.

What did the father of the computer send to the Library?

In 1851, Charles Babbage, inventor of the first mechanical calculator that later evolved into the modern computer, sent the Library a copy of his book *The Exposition of 1851, or, Views of the Industry, the Science, and the Government of England.*

Do librarians answer questions by telephone?

Staff of the National Reference Service provide telephone information and refer inquiries to other reading rooms (202-707-5522). For involved questions, it is best to write to: National Reference Service, Library of Congress, Washington, D.C. 20540-5570.

What are some other useful Library Internet addresses?

Library of Congress Web Site (gateway to Library services)
http://www.loc.gov/

Online Catalog
http://lcweb.loc.gov/catalog/

Reading Rooms and Information Centers
http://lcweb.loc.gov/rr/rrbrief.html

United States Copyright Office
http://lcweb.loc.gov/copyright/

Library Exhibitions
http://lcweb.loc.gov/exhibitions/

THOMAS: Legislative Information (information on congressional legislation)
http://thomas.loc.gov/

National Library Service for the Blind and Physically Handicapped
http://lcweb.loc.gov/nls/

Services for Persons with Disabilities
http://lcweb.loc.gov/visit/ada.html

L I B R A R Y   S T A F F

How many people work at the Library?

In 1852, a staff of five served the Library. Today, there are 4,194.

Who was the first woman appointed to an administrative position at the Library?

Jessica L. Farnum was appointed Secretary of the Library in 1906. It was a key position specially authorized by Congress. She was in charge of the Librarian's secretarial staff, mail, and messenger service. A later appointment was Florence Hellman who was named Acting Chief Bibliographer in 1930. Seven years later, she was made chief of her section. Miss Hellman was a regal woman who arrived in a chauffeured limousine each morning and on cold days wore her mink coat. She came from the Hellman mayonnaise family.

What presidential relative worked at the Library?

Lawrence Washington, great-great-grandson of George Washington's younger brother, John Augustine Washington, worked twenty-two years at the Library. He was custodian of the Senators' and Representatives' Reading Room. In recognition of his service to Congress, he was given a special tribute on February 23, 1920 as part of the birthday honors paid by the House to President Washington.

What staff member taught himself Chinese?

Berry Claytor, an African-American staff member with a law degree from Howard University, taught himself to read and write Chinese after volunteering to help bind Asian periodicals. Eventually, he was one of three staff members in charge of Chinese manuscripts and books. In 1919 after his return from U.S. Army service in France, he was permanently assigned to the Chinese Section.

What was J. Edgar Hoover's connection to the Library?

Hoover worked in the Library's Exchange and Gift Division from 1912 to 1917.

What staff member owned a Gutenberg Bible?

Arthur A. Houghton, Jr., was appointed curator of the Rare Book Division in 1940. He was president of Steuben Glass, Inc., and director of the Corning Glass Works. A collector of rare books, he owned a first folio of Shakespeare, the manuscript of *Boswell's Life of Samuel Johnson,* and a Gutenberg Bible.

Mr. Houghton made a rare gift to the Library in 1948. It was the congressional document ratifying the 13th Amendment to the Constitution abolishing slavery. Made of vellum, it bears the signatures of four authenticating officers of Congress and President Lincoln who approved it on February 1, 1865. The second half of the document bears the signatures of the representatives and senators who voted for it.

What is the Page School?

Young men and women of high-school age work as pages or messengers in both houses of Congress. The Page School holds classes from 6:30–9:30 a.m. Established in 1946, the school was originally located in the U.S. Capitol but, in September 1949, it moved to the Jefferson Building. The school was exclusively male until Congress admitted young women in 1971.

How are students selected?

Through recommendations by congressional representatives from their home districts.

Who was the first prominent African-American staff member?

Only six years after the abolition of slavery, the Library hired Daniel A. P. Murray, a seminary graduate. He was assigned to compile bibliographies and collect literature on African Americans. In 1900, he published a *Preliminary List of Books by Negro Authors, for the Paris Exposition and Library of Congress.* Murray helped organize an exhibition on blacks in Paris, served on President McKinley's inauguration committee, and was a delegate to the Republican National Convention. Few Library staff have surpassed Murray's fifty-two years of service. His total absence on account of illness in a twenty-five year period amounted to twenty-seven days. He retired on December 31, 1922. The poet Paul Laurence Dunbar worked with Murray in the Main Reading Room from 1897 to 1898.

What was the "Departmental Baseball League?"

The League was organized in 1905 by Thomas G. Alvord, Chief Clerk of the Library
It consisted of nine teams:

Library	*War*	*Post Office*
Interior	*Justice*	*Treasury*
Commerce and Labor	*Agriculture*	*Navy*

The colors of the Library team were Yale gray with blue trimmings and blue stockings.
The opening game was won by the Library 9–3 against Treasury. At the end of the
season, Navy was in first place and the Library in seventh.

Where do Library staff have to wear winter coats and gloves all year round?

In the film vaults at Landover, Maryland, where the temperature is kept at thirty-four
degrees. No one working in the vaults could bear the cold without protective clothing.

Who was the Library's first great linguist?

Louis C. Solyom was born in the Austro-Hungarian Empire in 1836 and came to the
United States in 1861. He enlisted in a New York regiment, fought in eleven battles with
the Army of the Potomac, was captured, and escaped by swimming the Rappahannock
River only to be later wounded at Chancellorsville. He settled in Washington and
worked in a bookstore, where he met Librarian Spofford who hired him to catalog
books. Solyom could speak French, German, Hungarian, Italian, Polish, Russian,
Slovak, Spanish, and Turkish. In addition, he could read Armenian, Bulgarian, Chinese,
Croatian, Dutch, and Persian. For his work with the Turkish collections, he was
awarded a gold medal by the sultan of Turkey in 1899. Solyom worked forty-six years
at the Library. His face was sculpted for the ethnic heads on the Jefferson Building
keystone. He is the only staff member featured in Library decoration.

How many staff members served during World War I?

About ninety-seven Library members, including two women who
went to France with the Red Cross. Four Library servicemen died in action.

How many staff members served during World War II?

About 424 Library men and women. Fifteen Library servicemen died in action.

What staff member served long enough to undo what he started?

In 1939, Leonard Harrison turned on the switch activating the Library's pneumatic tube system that carried books between buildings. When the system was shut down forty years later and replaced by an automatic book carrier, it was Harrison who turned off the old system.

What is the Library of Congress Time Capsule?

A project to remind library staff in 2100 what it was like to work at the Library in 2000.

What items will be included in the capsule?

Here is a sample:

American flag flown from the Capitol on April 24, 2000

Library flag

Piece of the Library's copper roof

Floor plans for all buildings

List of Jefferson books burned in 1851 and now being replaced

Photo of Madison Council Members and what their donations bought

Librarian Billington's personal letter listing the Library's greatest achievements

Library Billington's drugstore reading glasses

Library police badge

Library ID card

Lobby photographs showing X-ray equipment

Library organizational chart

Library phone directory

Staff breakdown by race

Library vacancy announcements

Library pay scale union bargaining agreements

Workstation photographs

Sample reference questions from each of the reading rooms

Employee's E-mail printouts

Ergonomic office supplies catalog

Employee descriptions of commuting

Carpool permit

Library snow emergency rules

Photographs showing typical work day

Employee descriptions of their jobs

Library newsletter

Copyright notice

Cafeteria menu

Library building photographs with cars passing

Area store photographs

Seeds from Capitol grounds dogwood trees that may be extinct by 2001

Library concert programs

Library art exhibit catalog

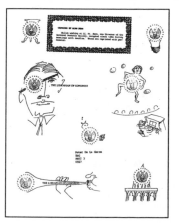

Even staff meetings inspire creativity, as seen in these Library doodles by Alan Fern, now Director of the National Portrait Gallery.

PRESERVATION

How are the fragile copies of the Gettysburg Address and other Top Treasures preserved?

Two state-of-the-art containers house these documents with stainless steel inner support and two outer frames that allow viewing from both sides through 1/4" Plexiglas. The containers are filled with low-moisture argon gas that has been purged of oxygen, thus preventing deterioration. The documents are suspended without adhesive support. They lie between two pieces of non-woven polyester sandwiched between window mats. These containers are the permanent home of the Gettysburg Address and will be constructed for the Library's other Top Treasures.

How does the Library preserve books that are turning brittle?

Books are put on a trolley holding more than a thousand volumes, placed in a large vacuum chamber, and exposed to the gas DEZ for about fifty hours to prolong their shelf life from 150 to 250 years.

Anti-Acid: In its deacidification facility at Fort Detrick, Maryland, the Library uses a huge vacuum chamber that previously tested materials for outer space. The process restores alkaline content to the paper and slows embrittlement. Book paper self-destructs because acid used in papermaking breaks down wood fibers, weakens the paper itself after 25–100 years, and eventually crumbles it to dust.

In 1996, around 25,000 books were treated. In 1997, almost 47,000 books were deacidified.

What is the Library facility at Wright-Patterson Air Force Base in Dayton, Ohio?

The base has a vault and laboratory where it preserves nitrate film, which is highly flammable. It also conducts the Library's gas DEZ treatment for preserving books.

How many items are in the Library of Congress?

This is the question most often asked by Library visitors: As of 1999, the Library had 119 million items in its collections. In 1992, the Library received its 100 millionth item.

How many miles of shelf space are there in Library buildings?

There are 2,807,775 linear feet or 532 miles of shelf space.

How much mail arrives at the Library each year?

About 22 million pieces of mail. An additional 2.6 million pieces arrive for separate processing by Copyright and the Exchange and Gift Division.

How much mail arrives at the Library each day?

About 80,000 pieces of mail.

What are the Library's major annual accomplishments?

In 1999, the Library:

welcomed nearly 2 million on-site visitors.

averaged 60 million monthly electronic transactions, including 8 million on the THOMAS legislative information system and 9 million on the American Memory Web site.

digitized 1.4 million files for the American Memory online historical collections.

How did the Library's book collections grow?

Year	Volumes
1800	243
1814	3,000
1830	16,000
1840	30,000
1863	79,000
1869 *	175,000
1870 **	237,000
1897	840,000
1899	900,000
1902	1,114,000
1910	1,800,000
1928	3,700,000
1940	6,000,000
1975	17,000,000
2000	19,000,000

* In 1866, around 40,000 volumes were added from the Smithsonian Institution

** In 1870, all copyright deposits were centralized at LC

What is the Library's budget?

The Library's budget for fiscal year 2000 is $419 million.

SELECTED BIBLIOGRAPHY

Ainsworth Rand Spofford: A Memorial Meeting at the Library of Congress on Thursday November 12, 1908. New York: Webster Press, 1909.

Annual Report of the Librarian of Congress. Washington, D.C.: Government Printing Office, Library of Congress, 1866– .

Ashley, Frederick W. *"The Library of Congress."* Typescript. Ashley Papers, Library of Congress Manuscript Division. Also available on microfilm.

Bishop, William Warner. *The Library of Congress.* Washington, D.C.: Government Printing Office, 1914

Bishop, William Warner and Andrew Keogh, eds. *Essays Offered to Herbert Putnam by his Colleagues and Friends on his Thirtieth Anniversary as Librarian of Congress, 5 April 1929. New Haven: Yale University Press, 1929;* reprint ed., Freeport, N.Y.: Books for Libraries Press, 1967.

Blashfield, Edwin Howland. *The Works of Edwin Howland Blashfield, with an Introduction by Royal Cortissoz.* New York: C. Scribner's Sons, 1937.

Cole, John Y. *Ainsworth Rand Spofford: Bookman and Librarian.* Littleton, Colorado: Libraries Unlimited, 1975.

Cole, John Y., ed. *For Congress and the Nation: A Chronological History of the Library of Congress.* Washington, D.C.: Library of Congress, 1979.

Cole, John Y. *Jefferson's Legacy: A Brief History of the Library of Congress.* Washington, D.C.: Library of Congress, 1993.

Cole, John Y. and Henry Hope Reed, eds. The Library of Congress: *The Art and Architecture of the Thomas Jefferson Building.* New York: W. W. Norton, 1997.

The Gazette. Library of Congress: A Weekly Newspaper for the Library Staff, 1990– .

Goodrum, Charles A. and Helen W. Dalrymple. *Guide to the Library of Congress.* Washington, D.C.: Library of Congress, 1982.

Goodrum, Charles A. *Treasures of the Library of Congress. New York:* H. N. Abrams, 1991.

Hilker, Helen-Anne. *Ten First Street, Southeast: Congress Builds a Library, 1886–1897.* Washington, D.C.: Library of Congress, 1980

Johnston, William Dawson. *History of the Library of Congress.* Vol. 1, 1800–1864. Washington, D.C.: Government Printing Office, 1904. [No further volumes published.]

Librarians of Congress, 1802–1974. Washington, D.C.: Library of Congress, 1977.

The Library of Congress: A Documentary History. Washington, D.C.: Congressional Information Service, 1987. [Microfilm of Library documents, annual reports, guides to collections, and inventories]

Library of Congress Archives. Manuscript Division. This collection contains the richest source of Library history. There are some 2.25 million items housed in 5,200 boxes. Also available are 261 microfilm reels that duplicate many of the items included in the 2.25 million count.

Library of Congress Information Bulletin, 1942–   .

Mearns, David C. *The Story Up to Now, 1800–1946. In Annual Report of the Librarian of Congress for the Fiscal Year Ending June 30, 1946.* Washington, D.C.: Government Printing Office, 1947; reprint ed., Boston: Gregg Press, 1972. Also printed separately, 1947.

Melville, Annette, comp. *Special Collections in the Library of Congress: A Selective Guide.* Washington, D.C.: Library of Congress, 1991.

Nelson, Josephus and Judith Farley. *Full Circle: Ninety Years of Service in the Main Reading Room.* Washington, D.C.: Library of Congress, 1980.

Pierson, Harriet Wheeler. Rosemary: *Reminiscences of the Library of Congress.* Washington, D.C., 1943.

Quarterly Journal of Accessions of the Library of Congress. 1943–1963. Title changed to *Quarterly Journal of the Library of Congress, 1964–1983.*

Rosenberg, Jane A. *The Nation's Great Library: Herbert Putnam and the Library of Congress, 1899–1939.* Urbana and Chicago: University of Illinois Press, 1993.

Salamanca, Lucy. *Fortress of Freedom: The Story of the Library of Congress.* Philadelphia: J. B. Lippincott, 1942.

Small, Herbert, comp. *Handbook of the New Library of Congress.* Boston: Curtis & Cameron, 1901; reprinted ed., Washington, D.C.: Library of Congress, 1980.